What Are They Saying About Environmental Ethics?

Pamela Smith

PAULIST PRESS
New York / Mahwah, N.J.

Cover design by James F. Brisson

Library of Congress Cataloging-in-Publication Data

Smith, Pamela.
    What are they saying about environmental ethics? / Pamela Smith.
      p. cm.
    Includes bibliographical references (p.)
    ISBN 0-8091-3754-2 (alk. paper)
    1. Environmental ethics.   2. Human ecology—Religious aspects.
3. Religion and science. I. Title.
GE42.S58   1997
179′.1—dc21   97-36615
                                                      CIP

Published by Paulist Press
997 Macarthur Boulevard
Mahwah, New Jersey 07430

Printed and bound in the
United States of America

Contents

Dedicated to
Ralph H. Starkey, M.D., endocrinologist,
and Janet Tomcavage, R.N., diabetes nurse practitioner,
for their continued efforts at
promoting health and quality of life
for their diabetic patients

Introduction

In the last decades of the twentieth century, citizens of Times Beach, Missouri, Bhopal, India, and Chernobyl, Ukraine, have faced evacuation and death because of environmental disasters. Meteorologists and skywatchers have reported holes in the Earth's protective ozone layer and have noted the consequent threat of skin cancer and blindness. Meanwhile, summertime warnings go out about the escalation in ground-level ozone production and its particular hazards to the old, the very young, the asthmatic, and those with other respiratory conditions. Astronauts and cosmonauts have extolled the fragile, stunning beauty of the "blue planet" while also alerting Earth's inhabitants to the fact that the devastation of rain forests and the conflagration of burning Mid-East oil wells prove visible even far above the Earth. Siberian sands along the Yenisey River are said to be contaminated with plutonium, and traces of temperate-zone pesticides have been found in the pancreases of Antarctic penguins. In 1993 the Physicians for Social Responsibility, a group initially founded to sound the alarm about the grave medical hazards of nuclear weaponry and nuclear warfare, pronounced their diagnosis of the state of the planet's health. They found Earth to be, largely for environmental reasons, languishing in *Critical Condition*.[1]

A number of governmental agencies and a proliferation of nongovernmental organizations have been founded in response to the growing awareness that air, water, and soil can be and have been contaminated and that rare, precious species of wildlife have been driven into extinction. Exotic forms of flora have disappeared as forests have been clear-cut and agribusinesses have advanced monoculture farming. New terms like "biodiversity" have appeared in human parlance as ecologists (scientists) and environmentalists (advocates for the environment in humanitarian, philosophical, or political veins) have raised an outcry on behalf of Earth-saving and Earth-healing.

The seriousness of the threat to the human environment has led the Catholic bishops of the Philippines to proclaim the preservation of the Earth, its resources and its richly varied species the "ultimate pro-life issue."[2] Groups from Worldwatch to the World Council of Churches have demanded the deliberate development of an ethic of environmental "sustainability."[3] American Vice President Al Gore, in his acclaimed *Earth in the Balance,* has urged a conscientious examination of "the habits of mind and action" which have led to the latter twentieth-century environmental crisis.[4] And a host of deep ecologists, ecofeminists, naturalists, liberationists, conservationists, animal rights activists, philosophical ethicists, and religionists have issued a moral call for drastic attitudinal and behavioral change vis-à-vis the natural world.

Increases in recycling and decreases in fur-wearing appear to be among the observable results of the environmental movement. A popular demand for environmentally responsible corporate behavior seems to be gaining ground. An academic and religious response to often disturbing and startling environmental information is also underway. In recent decades new fields of inquiry and discussion have appeared: ecotheology, ecospirituality and creation spirituality, ecophilosophy, and environmental ethics. The last of these, environmental ethics, while still very much in a developmental phase, has already been recognized by the Society of Christian Ethics as an area of specialization and has appeared in the undergraduate and graduate offerings of philosophy and religion departments at a number of colleges and universities. The philosophical journal *Environmental Ethics* has, from its inception in 1979, been a forum for discussion of methodological issues, semantic questions, axiomatic foundations, and applications in the "ought" and "ought not" realm of environmental ethics. Other philosophical and theological journals are increasingly carrying eco-ethical articles and notes.

Environmental ethics as a field of moral inquiry seems, then, to be coming into its own. As what is sometimes a cacophony of voices have been raised, a number of issues have repeatedly appeared. Aside from a broad consensus that "sustainability" is a worthy goal for moral agents, the opinions put forth on a variety of pertinent issues and related questions are, not surprisingly, widely diverse.

Most critical among these ethical issues would seem to be the following:

1) What overall vision of the natural world is the most fitting and salutary: anthropocentrism? biocentrism? ecocentrism?
2) Do beings and things other than humans have "intrinsic value," or are they more properly assigned "instrumental value"?
3) Can animals, plant life, land, seas, ecosystems, or nature in general—some of these, or all of these—be said to have "rights"?
4) Do humans have moral obligations to any beings other than persons now existent? That is, can there be obligations to not yet born or not yet apparent beings?
5) What is the proper *telos* of human interaction with other living species and the nonliving world?
6) What specific moral choices concerning the Earth environment and its various living beings can be prescribed and proscribed?

The book which follows presents a survey of the responses to these and other related questions offered by the more significant emergent schools of environmental ethical thought. **Chapter 1** considers one of the most radical philosophical approaches, that of **deep ecology. Chapter 2** samples the growing body of **ecofeminist** literature. **Chapter 3** surveys the philosophical grounding and the ethical conclusions of the **animal rights** movement. **Chapter 4** synthesizes the ecocentric thought of the Aldo Leopold school, here referred to as the **naturalist** approach. **Chapter 5** presents the dominant themes of **liberationist** reflection, which correlates environmental issues with Third World poverty and liberation theology. **Chapter 6** highlights the declarations of **interreligious and ecumenical** voices, focusing on the Parliament of the World's Religions and the World Council of Churches. In **Chapter 7,** the eco-ethical themes appearing in contemporary **Catholic magisterial** statements are surveyed. And, finally, **Chapter 8** draws some conclusions about the directions and divergencies of environmental ethical thought.

In 1975 philosopher Holmes Rolston III raised the question, "Is There an Ecological Ethic?" The essay addressed the question of how a life science, ecology, might interact constructively with ethics.[5] The "WATSA" book which follows presumes, like the schools of thought it presents, that scientific fact-gathering and accurate ecological information are critical to the processes of ethical reflection and moral discernment. But it also presumes that a whole array of abstract concepts like values, virtues, moral considerability, moral good, moral evil, rightness and wrongness are beyond the capacity of the science of ecology to address. Thus it refers to the field as environmental ethics, which seems to be the more standard choice and less likely to imply what Joseph Des Jardins calls an "overreliance on science and technology" in ethical discussion.[6] It has to be acknowledged, however, that "ecological ethics" and "eco-ethics" are used variously—sometimes to suggest a purposefully ecocentric worldview; at other times simply as synonymous variants for "environmental ethics." In this text, the synonymous use will appear occasionally for stylistic reasons.

As will be evident from what follows, environmental ethics draws deeply upon philosophical and religious resources while also attending to science, history, economics, and politics. Van Rensselaer Potter, the coiner of the term "bioethics," which has come to be used almost exclusively with reference to medical ethics, insists that a "global bioethics," an ethics that links human health to the health of the whole natural environment, is today imperative—that it is indeed the only route to insuring "acceptable survival."[7] Whatever their persuasions and variations, it seems safe to say that all of the schools of thought presented in these chapters are engaged in the project of formulating an ethic which chooses life, promotes its quality, and defends the entirety of the living Earth against violence and death.

1
Deep Ecology and Its Radical Vision

Arne Naess, the originator of the term "deep ecology" and the philosophical progenitor of the green deep ecology "movement,"[1] can be said, in a sense, to have offered initially more a prolegomenon to practical environmental ethics than a well-developed applied eco-ethical system. Naess, a Spinoza scholar and a proponent of Gandhian nonviolence,[2] has proffered this disclaimer: "I'm not much interested in ethics or morals. I'm interested in how we experience the world.... If you articulate your experience then it can be a philosophy or religion."[3] The protestation notwithstanding, it is precisely in developing his "philosophy" of world-experience, the philosophy which he calls "Ecosophy T," that Naess, with like-minded environmental philosophers, has proposed, in a quarter century of "deep ecology" work, a theory of "self-realization" and "wide identification" which is both a "vision" and a moral-ethical "platform." The vision is biocentric, radically egalitarian, and sometimes polemic. The "platform" is a set of general principles and practical maxims which are meant to guide individual human behaviors and socio-political decisions concerning the environment.

"Ecosophy T" is the designation which Naess has used for his vision of multilateral "intrinsic value," the good of biodiversity, and a relational, ecological philosophic anthropology. Naess develops in Ecosophy T, David Rothenberg says, "a new ontology," a perception of being-in-the-world which resists Western philosophy's tendency to separate the human from other species and counters the West's predilection to hierarchical thinking and the preferential treatment of human wants and interests.[4]

5

An Exposition of "Ecosophy T"

In the early 1970s, as a direct response to the signs of environmental crisis then looming, Naess offered Ecosophy T as a model for the development of other ecophilosophies. His system was called an "ecosophy" as a kind of shorthand for ecology and ecocentric philosophy but also as a kind of proposal for *oikos* and *sophos:* wisdom about the planetary "dwelling place."[5] He appended the letter "T" for "Tvergastein," his rustic Norwegian cabin and retreat, suggesting that any and all ecophilosophies must be envisioned from a concrete locale, a locale that is familiar to the philosopher and with which she or he has a personal relationship.[6]

Naess describes his "ecosophy" as largely intuitive,[7] though it has an empirical basis in the contemporary cosmological, evolutionary worldview.[8] For Naess, what a general grasp of cosmogenesis and biogenesis leads to is a recognition of the "autotelic value" of all species and lifeforms.[9] The first perception of deep ecology is that humans can no longer be thought of as belonging to a species which makes them exclusively ends-in-themselves. Instead, all living beings must be regarded as ends-in-themselves, possessed of unique drives and purposefulness.

Naess sees inscribed in nature the primary drive to "Self-realization!" This "Self-realization!" is, in fact, the first of thirteen "ultimate norms" of ecosophy which he has enumerated.[10] Linked to these norms are a set of fifteen "hypotheses," some of which hardly seem hypothetical (e.g., "H 12: Exploitation reduces or eliminates potentials").[11] The norms formulated by Naess are exclamatory, suggesting that they are imperatives, though not in all cases exceptionless.[12] The norms are as follows:

N 1: Self-realization!
N 2: Self-realization for all living beings!
N 3: Diversity of life!
N 4: Complexity!
N 5: Symbiosis!
N 6: Local self-sufficiency and cooperation!
N 7: Local autonomy!
N 8: No centralization!
N 9: No exploitation!
N 10: No subjection!

N   11:   All have equal rights to Self-realization!
N   12:   No class societies!
N   13:   Self-determination![13]

What Naess is suggesting by these imperatives or "norms" is that a healthful, realistic, reasonable ecophilosophy will apprehend "intrinsic value" in all beings[14] and will perceive diversity, complexity, locality, and what he terms "biospherical egalitarianism"[15] as goods. The ethical extension of such an "ecosophy" will translate into choices for the protection of pan-species flourishing. It will prize relationality— i.e., symbiotic interrelatedness and interdependence[16]—and emphasize bioregional ("local") environmental decision making. It will favor decentralized, nonexploitative, classless social structures. Naess recalls that the first norm, as noted earlier, "expresses an ontology," while the set of norms as a whole articulate a "deontology," a set of duties or values which ought to be fostered and preserved.[17]

Key to Naess's "ecosophy" is his expansive notion of the "self," a "Self...that expands from each of us to include all."[18] For Naess, the sea, dunes, beach grass, bayberry, gulls, mosquitoes, clamshells, mussels, seaweed, osprey nests, and sunsets over a bay are all part of the "Self" of a resident of a New Jersey barrier island—if, that is, the island has not been altogether altered and defaced by weekenders, summer people, and boardwalk entrepreneurs. The "Self" is not one that swallows all of these lifeforms up acquisitively and possessively, but rather it is one that identifies with them, recognizing that these creatures and features are part of oneself and that one is part of a whole of life, a local living system. For Naess, all of these parts have "equal status," whether human or nonhuman.[19]

This view of the "Self" underlying Ecosophy T, and thus deep ecology, clearly makes deep ecology stridently non-anthropocentric. Humanity is not "subordinated" to the nonhuman, writers in the field assert in response to criticisms which have suggested that humans are too displaced from deep ecology's consideration. Instead, deep ecologists claim, humans are challenged to move from the egocentric to the ecocentric in their choices.[20]

It should be noted here that earlier summaries of deep ecology labeled its non-anthropocentrism "biocentric," while more recent presentations have used the term "biospheric," which seems more intentionally synonymous with "ecocentric." There is a certain persistent indefiniteness about the shift—an indefiniteness due in part to Naess's own propensity to resist "precisations" and allow "many parallel interpretations" of his thought.[21] The earlier use of "biocentrism" has apparently led some environmental thinkers to ally themselves more with those treated in this text (Chapter 4) as the "naturalists," or "environmental holists," who more definitively include the land and landforms, and not only fauna and flora, as central to moral consideration.

Along with Naess's resistance to "precision," another reason for indefiniteness or indistinction about adverting to a "biocentric" or "biospheric" worldview may be the fact that, since the popularization of the Gaia hypothesis, there has been a marked tendency among environmental thinkers to regard the planet as a whole as a living system, and so too the various ecosystems or bioregions.[22] Rocks, crystals, grains of sand, and the most seemingly nonliving things have come to be perceived as integrally part of living systems. "Intricate, living diversity" is, says Naess, the focus of deep ecology,[23] so it does seem honest, though it may be somewhat confusing, to call this school of thought either "biocentric" or "ecocentric." The interchangeable, though imprecise, usage persists not only in the "philosophy" but also in the "movement."

The Deep Ecology "Platform"

Australian Warwick Fox, developing what he terms "transpersonal ecology," and Americans Bill Devall and George Sessions have been at the forefront of the movement to refine and elaborate on the theoretical and practical bases for deep ecology as an ethical counterforce to what Naess has termed "shallow ecology." "Shallow ecology" is understood to be that personal and political view which, in its entrenched anthropocentrism, regards the natural world and its various species merely as resources "for us" and ascribes value instrumentally—on the basis of service to human interests, often very short-range ones.[24]

By the mid-1980s, Naess had joined with George Sessions to formulate what they termed a "platform" for deep ecology, eight oft-reprinted proposals which Naess has described as an "axiology" as opposed to the ontology-deontology of his norms.[25] The eight points of the "platform" can be summarized thus:

1) Recognition of the equal intrinsic value of all beings;
2) Affirmation of multiplicity, diversity, and complexity as values in themselves;
3) Permissibility of human use or killing of living beings or disruption of the environment solely to meet vital needs;
4) Decrease in human population;
5) Acknowledgment that humans are at present inhibiting and violating vital life processes;
6) Profound socio-economic policy changes based on cultural-philosophical changes as a counteraction to ecologically damaging practices and mindsets;
7) Emphasis on "life quality" rather than on "standard of living";
8) Moral obligation to action on the part of all who affirm platform principles 1–7.[26]

Alan Drengson and Yuichi Inoue have observed that a variety of green party members and eco-activists give their allegiance to these and like principles. It seems inevitable that, given the proposal of a "platform," deep ecology would become associated with the efforts of Greenpeace, EarthFirst!, and such groups. Questions of misanthropy and also questions of tactics have, not surprisingly, arisen as certain activists have engaged in bitter confrontations and others have justified acts of eco-sabotage as "eco-defense."[27]

The charge of deep ecology's misanthropy has arisen, first of all, from its "biocentric/biospheric egalitarianism" and ambiguities about the application of such egalitarianism, then from its disdainful attitude toward "progress" and technological "development," and, finally, from its negativity toward the human population count (including a much-quoted Naess observation that the maximal human count for the whole planet ought to be 100 million).[28] While Naess resists being adamant or absolutist about his prescriptions, he makes it clear that his Ecosophy T perceives far less than zero population growth as a desirable goal and foresees a need for radical rethinking and restructuring of human lifestyles and cultures as the route to reversing "a crisis of consumerism."[29]

Other figures in the deep ecology movement have been less irenic than Naess has in their critique of population patterns and public policy.

An EarthFirst! columnist, for example, has often been cited for a notorious remark in the face of the onslaught of AIDS:

> I take it as axiomatic that the only real hope for the continuation of diverse ecosystems on this planet is an enormous decline in human population.... [I]f the AIDS epidemic didn't exist, radical environmentalists would have to invent one.[30]

Comments along these lines, as well as some tactical maneuvers by "radical environmentalists," have led other environmental thinkers, like Al Gore, to remark that some of those who stand on the deep ecology platform seem to regard human beings as "an alien presence on the earth."[31]

Certain standoffs against what may be judged less than "vital" human interference with the environment have also invited critique. A classic episode is recounted by Roderick Nash, author of *The Rights of Nature*. In 1979, Mark Dubois, an environmental activist, chained himself to a cliff in the Stanislaus River Canyon at a site unknown to the army engineers who were charged with the task of flooding the canyon in a dam-building and reservoir-filling project. His life was spared when the engineers, failing to locate him and release him, had to halt the reservoir-filling proceedings. Dubois described his action, and the risk of his own life, as a "personal expression of love for a river and a non-violent way of protesting a moral wrong."[32] Since the Dubois-army affair, numerous confrontations between activists and governmental, agricultural, or entrepreneurial agencies have been recounted in the news media.

Deep ecology continues to be challenged to face questions about the appropriateness of such actions and the degree of radical commitment required to protect the "Self-realization!" of creatures and canyons. It also continues to be challenged to set forth principles to guide determinations for the negotiation of competing interests and the resolution of moral dilemmas.

To address such perplexities, Naess has proposed as guidelines what might be called principles of priority and nearness. "The more vital interest has priority over the less vital," Naess declares, and "the nearer has priority over the more remote—in space, time, culture, species."[33] The interests of muskrats and marigolds in surviving and thriving override the interests of mall mobbers in search of more parking spaces, then. But how is the principle of "nearness" applied? The immediate need for a water supply for living human beings might arguably take precedence over the need of future generations for a beauteous canyon. The fact that one man "loves" a canyon and that numerous nonhuman lifeforms will be dealt death, while others suffer the loss of habitat, may, however, be judged as taking precedence over the need for water, especially if water consumption is extravagant and excessive. In the Stanislaus River Canyon case, it is hard to determine which needs or interests ought, in the end, to take priority. And it is hard to determine whether the army engineers ought to feel more "nearness" to Dubois or to the proposed beneficiaries of the reservoir.

Deep ecology's anti-hierarchical position, holding the essential parity of species, makes it difficult to determine, then, what interests count as more "vital" and what beings are "nearer." Do the interests of spotted owls and Canadian geese necessarily take precedence over the interests of zebras and elephants for North Americans? Are the interests of Michigan ferns and lakes more pressing than the interests of Amazon rain forests to the person who lives "nearer" to Michigan? Is the diabetic family dachshund more deserving of investment and medical support than an anonymous aging Appalachian diabetic human? Paul Taylor asserts that, given the "impartiality" of deep ecology, "the killing of a wildflower, then, when taken in and of itself, is just as much a wrong, other things being equal, as the killing of a human....In some situations, it is a *greater* wrong to kill a wildflower than it is, in another situation, to kill a human."[34]

While this kind of premise pervades writings in deep ecology and in the green "movement," it is difficult to find descriptions, case studies, or exempla adequate to determine what "situations" render one wrongful killing graver than another or what conditions render things "equal" such that the killing of a member of one species becomes as reprehensible as the killing of another. Questions of competing interests and demands for impartiality in the rendering of environmental decisions turn on the questions of "rights"—and the ancillary questions of whether, in an anti-hierarchical vision, any "rights" can clearly be established as having priority.

The Rights Question

Arne Naess has declared that his Ecosophy T, by ascribing "intrinsic value to all living beings," is thus asserting a "right to live" for all beings.[35] As the deep ecology movement has developed, it has, then, asserted a notion of rights which subsumes and supersedes several centuries of development in *human* rights theorizing. Deep ecology suggests that rights are not only the possession of human moral agents—of, that is, rational, articulate, ethically responsible beings— but also of beings which can be affected by moral agents. The "right to live" and to flourish is understood to be held by "moral patients," recipients of moral-ethical decisions, and status as a "moral patient" is accorded to all beings.[36] The "right to live" is not absolute, but the suspension of that right for any being must be subjected to stricter standards, argue deep ecologists.

In 1974 Christopher Stone published *Should Trees Have Standing? Toward Legal Rights for Natural Objects.* The first part of the text argues that at one time it was unthinkable to consider women or children as possessors of rights. Pointing to developments in rights thinking that have made the unthinkable not only thinkable but a matter of law, Stone suggests that there are now solid legal precedents for regarding nonhuman beings and natural entities as rights holders. The second part of Stone's study is a record of legal cases, including U.S. Supreme Court cases, in which natural entities like river valleys and wildernesses have "won" the "right" to remain unmolested.[37]

In a similar vein, Roderick Frazier Nash traces the development of the "natural rights" theory which has been applied in Anglo-Saxon law and jurisprudence. He perceives an ever-widening conception of legal rights-bearing. Citing a chronology which begins with the Magna Carta and the protection of the interests and "rights" of English barons, Nash notes that male American colonists, then slaves, then women, then children and laborers and blacks and Native Americans and, finally, he believes, "nature" have been accorded rights.[38] Nash notes that preparation for the success of "rights of nature" claims was made by a host of environmental writers, including some (John Muir, Aldo Leopold) whose work preceded by many decades the contemporary environmental movement.[39]

Speaking matter-of-factly about "rights" of nonhuman beings and their habitats is a hallmark of the deep ecology movement. John Tallmadge has argued that the "spiritual" foundation of the ability to see nonhumans so interrelationally can be found in the cultivation of what he calls (after Martin Buber) an "I-You" approach or "attitude" which establishes "another mode of relation between us and the world."[40] What Tallmadge describes is a relationship in which "another being [is] encountered in its intrinsic wholeness," and thus "a relation of true equality (or, to use Buber's term, *reciprocity*)" is established.[41] Tall madge elaborates on the encounter and the recognition of relationality as a kind of Zen moment. He also, without crediting Naess, subscribes to the conviction that the sense of "self" has the potential for expansion—an expansion which it ought to have. "We need to reemphasize the 'personhood' of the land and the beings which live with it," he declares, and, in so doing, overcome the "pathological alienation" and separation which culture, custom, and hierarchical thinking have inculcated in our sense of selves.[42] A meditative, contemplative discipline is necessary, Tallmadge suggests, to attain an "I-You" regard for nonhuman beings. The practice of such a discipline will result in the ability to relate along the lines of what Naess has called "wide identification." And an outcome of this discipline will be a reverence for every being's desert of "Self-realization," though it should be added that Tallmadge does not use this Naess term per se.[43]

Tallmadge's mysticism is much like that with which every anthology of deep ecology seems charged—Zen or Native American or animist experiences which open the human person to a "relational event," an encounter, with the nonhuman world. This mysticism, as much as the kind of rights reasoning found in Stone and Nash, is often at the foundation of deep ecology and, in fact, is a considerable influence on Naess himself, whose Tvergastein moments and incursions into Eastern religious thought are as vital to Ecosophy T as his training in philosophy is.

Like Naess's principle of "nearness," Tallmadge's "I-You" ethic of human-nature relations has come in for attack. John Kultgen charges that "the core of morality" and thus of any ethic or special type of ethics (like environmental ethics) must be grounded in "respect for persons as persons and the consideration of their interests on a par with one's own."[44] For Kultgen, the treatment of "subpersons" as persons serves only to add hopeless confusion to the project of morality and to the making of ethical distinctions and determinations. While Kultgen wholeheartedly supports the appropriateness of moral "consideration" for all beings, he insists that only the parity of humans can ground moral discourse and indeed justice.[45]

Talk of "rights" and parity and of "I-You" relations with the land and creatures points again to the difficulty of resolving hard cases faced in environmental decision-making. There seem to be no clear standards for applying "biospheric egalitarianism" when rights conflict. Like Naess's elusive principles of "priority" and "nearness," Tallmadge's "I-You" relationality leaves the deep ecology adherent with no strategies for conflict resolution. He simply acknowledges that the pressure of need inevitably results in this situation for the human: "the You we encounter in some being in nature must always collapse into an It sooner or later."[46] He offers no suggestion as to when this "collapse" should be allowed. He merely advises that "symbiotic arrangements" be made as humans determine that they must kill, consume, or constrain other beings. The model he proposes is a "relation to the biosphere similar to that between the plains Indians and the buffalo." The buffalo was a "You," even "a god," Tallmadge claims, and yet could be used as an "it" for "food, clothing, fuel, and tools for the tribe."[47] Ceremonials and a sustained reverence for the spirits of the buffalo were, Tallmadge suggests, integral to symbiosis.

William French, who agrees with deep ecology's move toward "expansion of what counts as the moral community," asserts, however, that "[b]iospherical egalitarian claims…tend to be developed inconsistently and often do not *in fact* govern the concrete moral reasoning of even the theorists who most strongly espouse such beliefs."[48] The inconsistency which French perceives and describes in Naess and Paul Taylor arises from the "utopian" nature of the egalitarian ethic which so dooms it that it "fails to provide normative guidance in decision and action."[49] Given the difficulty of establishing standards for "normative guidance" in deep ecology, it is not surprising to find that, after the generalizations, many thinkers in this school of thought resort to proposing ideals for lifestyle alteration.

Peter Wenz, the author of *Environmental Justice,* is more a Leopoldian (see Chapter 4) than a deep ecologist. He has, however, some notable affinities with the Naess school. Wenz recommends that, on behalf of the besieged environment, people ought to practice what he terms "the principle of anticipatory cooperation (PAC). The PAC requires that under conditions of significant injustice, my behavior be somewhat better than that of people who are similar to me in relevant respects."[50] What this "PAC" requires is some deferral to the interests of creatures and landforms, even at some personal cost or inconvenience. It also implies the curtailment of certain human customs and preferences, particularly those which appear to assault other living beings unnecessarily. Meat-eating and the development of desert areas for housing would seem to be among the dubious activities which might be suspended if one were to practice the "PAC."

What Wenz proposes is what many writers on deep ecology enact in their lives: the adoption of transformed, counter-cultural ways of living and valuing as an intentional counteraction to what they adjudge the consumerist, materialist, mechanistic, technocratic mindsets abroad in their societal milieux. Poet Gary Snyder, ritualist Dolores La Chapelle, mountain climber Jack Turner, and media critic Jerry Mander (author of *Four Arguments for the Elimination of Television*) are among the frequent contributors to deep ecology anthologies whose personal lifestyles are renunciatory and markedly eco-conscious.[51] Each would seem, in his or her own way, to advocate the establishment of attentive, deliberate relationships with one's own natural surroundings. Each would follow more reverently the dictates of sunups and sundowns, moon phases and seasons. Each would jettison much of the clutter and gadgetry of modern "civilization." And each would take a non-utilitarian view of the variety of lifeforms and landforms, seeking harmony and cooperation rather than manipulation and exploitation. In pursuit of "wide identification," each develops what Warwick Fox calls a "transpersonal ecology," an ecology that promotes "the realization of a sense of self that extends beyond…one's egoic, biographical, or personal sense of self"[52] to move toward an appreciative, non-hierarchical vision of life "as a luxuriously branching bush, not as a linear scale that is filled in by greater and lesser examples of some ideal end point."[53] According to Fox (and to Snyder, La Chapelle, Turner, Mander, et al., it seems), humanity's readiness to promote "Self-realization!" in an egalitarian, impartial way will be achieved not by the formulation of "moral *injunctions*" but by the extension of "experiential *invitations*," as Fox terms them.[54]

Thus, while talking universal "rights," deep ecologists will perhaps be found as often reflecting on wildness, wilderness, and "the place of joy in a world of fact" as on the methodologies and structurings of deep ecological ethics.[55] They maintain Naess's thirteen norms as something of an axiology and the eight points of the Naess and Sessions "platform" as the primer for ethical action. But they resist delivering detailed prescriptions or a casuistry of deep ecology. For deep ecologists, it seems, ethical behavior vis-à-vis the environment is more a way of being than of doing. As such, it seems more mystical than moralistic.

Responses to Deep Ecology

The multiple schools of contemporary eco-ethical thought all have, in some way, to be measured against the backdrop of deep ecology since they can be seen as variations on deep ecology's themes or as alternatives to and even opponents of deep ecology.

Against deep ecology's anti-anthropocentric stance, Ann Arbor philosopher Henryk Skolimowski has proposed an "ecological humanism" which argues not for the "intrinsic value" of all species but instead for a rediscovery of the "intrinsic *values*" held in religious and philosophical traditions which can aid the human quest to "define ourselves as self-transcending beings."[56] Skolimowski believes that the reclaiming of such values can overcome "mere abstract, atomistic, analytical thinking" and "provide a new metaphysics."[57] This new perception of the ultimate nature of reality can be, Skolimowski urges, more respectful of life and more "life-enhancing," more spiritually alert and wisdom-seeking, more "comprehensive and global," and thus more aware of the good which ought to be done to advance the health of the planet and general "well-being."[58]

Like Naess, Skolimowski is convinced that it is critical to human self-understanding that human beings have a sense of place in the larger (and humbling) web of planetary and cosmic life. Unlike Naess, Skolimowski is confident that a sound, scientifically informed philosophical anthropology will incline humans not to a shocked recognition of their equivalence with all creatures but, rather, with a sense of themselves "as a part of and an extension of the evolving cosmos" which is uniquely endowed with "sanctity."[59] The human has an irrevocable "exquisiteness," argues Skolimowski, which renders human quality "more precious than the exquisiteness of the mosquito."[60] A type of process philosopher influenced by the thought of Teilhard de Chardin,[61] Skolimowski argues that an elevation, rather than an equalization, of human esteem for the human in relation to other beings and a perception of the directionality of evolution toward the human should actually lead to more life-affirming relations with the natural world.

Without taking Skolimowski's spiritual, Teilhardian turn, philosopher Bryan Norton would seem to concur with much in Skolimowski. Norton advocates a "weak anthropocentrism" which rests on "nonindividualistic" presuppositions.[62] Like Skolimowski, Norton finds the discussion of human values more profitable than the designation of "intrinsic value" for nonhumans. Norton argues that human "preferences" can be educated and evaluated ethically in such a way that the natural environment is given more consideration and more kindly treatment. For Norton, this formational approach to preferences (by a kind of "values clarification" process perhaps) requires neither a perception of self as complex culmination of an evolutionary trend nor, necessarily, the "wide identification" ideal of deep ecology. It merely requires more information and a more profound understanding of interrelatedness.

Thomas Derr, like Skolimowski, proposes that a renewed humanism, in this case a specifically "Christian humanism," is the route to responsible living in the Earth environment. Countering not only deep ecology's anti-anthropocentric tones but also what he perceives as a general unfriendliness to the Judaeo-Christian tradition characteristic of environmental ethical thought, Derr claims that an obediential reading and application of the biblical notion of stewardship can lead to positive care for and even "service to" creation and prudential use of its multiplex species and phenomena.[63] Derr, who regards himself as a nature-lover and a long-term environmentalist, objects to what he considers a certain presumptiveness in biocentric ethics about a great unknown, "nature's divine destiny."[64] He takes issue with Norton's "weak"/"strong" construct and insists that what is really needed is a "'wise-use' environmental ethic," a "smart anthropocentrism."[65]

As is evident, deep ecology, with its radical challenge to the primacy of place of the human and to the practices of "technocracy," has promoted much discussion of hierarchicalism, much reconsideration of notions of value, and much reexamination of priorities in ethical decision-making concerning the natural world. In response to deep ecology's promulgation of a non-anthropocentric vision, several schools of thought have developed an "ecocentrism" which does not altogether decenter the human, as subsequent chapters will show.

Some philosophers have reasserted anthropocentrism, but in the form of a new "humanism."

Another school of thought, one which shares many key concepts with deep ecology, is the one which identifies not anthropocentrism but androcentrism as the bedeviling force which has wrought havoc on the environment. As the thought of "ecofeminism" is now turned to, the question of whether it promotes "ecocentrism" in the mode of "biospheric egalitarianism" or a new anthropocentrism in the form of gynocentrism—a charge implied by Warwick Fox[66]—may be carried forward.

2
The Ethics of Ecofeminism

For ecofeminists, the way to the attainment of more harmonious interactions between humans and the Earth environment is not simply a matter of establishing more egalitarian relations; it is also a matter of retrieving a sense of the sacred. Ecofeminists decry repeatedly the "desacralization" of the natural world as one of the major factors contributing to the Western industrial nations' environmental abuses.[1] With the loss of a sense of the sacred—or perhaps with the loss of many kinds of nature mysticism—has come too the demise of the "organic" view of the planet and its multiform creatures.

The term "ecoféminisme" was first coined by Françoise d'Eaubonne and introduced to the English-speaking world in 1974.[2] According to Karen Warren, ecological feminism was born of an awareness of "women's potential for bringing about an ecological revolution" and a conviction that the illogic of "the logic of domination" must be exposed and the harms of "the twin dominations of women and nature" undone.[3] As Warren sees it, the mindset and the manipulations that effect racism, classism, sexism, and environmental abuse are of a piece. As is quite consistently noted,[4] ecofeminism addresses the complexities of oppressive, despoiling structures not so much by asserting rights as by emphasizing relationships. Ariel Salleh links ecofeminism to deep ecology in its adoption of "a *relational total-field* image" of the human and nature, its "biological egalitarianism," its "principle of diversity and symbiosis," its "anti-class posture," and its opposition to environmentally destructive activity.[5] Yet she critiques Naess and deep ecology at large as too vague, too academic, too jargon-ridden, and too blithely oblivious to the patriarchal roots of environmental damages.

For ecofeminists in general, the source of ecodestruction is not merely anthropocentrism; it is androcentrism, the predominance of the masculine and macho, in societal construction and norm-making. Perhaps the most thorough exposition of this theory of the historical links between androcentrism and environmental degradation is Carolyn Merchant's *The Death of Nature.* Merchant recounts how transformations in the philosophy of science led to the supplanting of "the image of an organic cosmos with a living female earth at its center" by "a mechanistic world view in which nature was reconstructed as dead and passive, to be dominated and controlled by humans."[6] The first view she roots in ancient philosophies and religions, reinforced by the Thomistic-scholastic system of the Middle Ages. The second view she associates with the dualistic philosophies of such English and French theorists as Francis Bacon, Marin Marsenne, Pierre Gassendi, René Descartes, Thomas Hobbes, and Isaac Newton, whose ideas overtook the traditional view of "cosmos" in the sixteenth, seventeenth, and eighteenth centuries.[7]

While Merchant shows that the organic view and the feminization of *natura* were not without ambiguities,[8] these were far preferable, she believes, to the mathematical, techno-mechanical, scientific view which, coupled with the upsurge of an individualistic, atomistic political anthropology, increasingly emphasized the conquest of nature. Despite some resistance from proposals of "organic utopias" like Tommaso Campanella's 1602 *City of the Sun* or Johann Valentin Andrea's *Christianopolis,* what Merchant regards as the rapacious vision of Francis Bacon's 1627 *New Atlantis* seems to have triumphed.[9] The age of technocratic science had begun and with it, Merchant believes, the ecological ruins which have become increasingly evident in the latter twentieth century. The only hope for new life is, as Merchant sees it, a new vision and such behavioral change as might occur with "the conjunction of the women's movement with the ecology movement."[10]

As historical models for the present day ecofeminist movement, Merchant highlights the Quaker philosopher and "vitalist" Lady Anne Conway, a friend of von Leibniz. She catalogues a number of women preachers, prominent intellectuals, and types of the "scientific lady" (like Margaret Cavendish, Duchess of Newcastle) who were activists for educational rights and religious leadership for women and for a scientific approach which was persuaded that "there was nothing dead or fallow in the universe."[11] Merchant's own work, since *The Death of Nature,* has focused on tracing the progress of the environmental movement and recounting the deeds of its participants.[12]

In *Radical Ecology,* Merchant suggests that what is needed is "an alternative vision of the world in which race, class, sex, and age barriers have been eliminated and basic human needs have been fulfilled."[13] Merchant clearly does not discount the significance of human concerns. However, she enumerates, among the contributions of a number of "radical" approaches to ecological ethics, their concerns for forests, endangered species, animals, fish, and cultivated fields. Without committing herself to a "biocentric" or "egalitarian" vision, Merchant asserts clearly her feminist and "organic" view. She also lauds the development of "[a]lternative, nonpatriarchal forms of spirituality and alternative pathways within mainstream religions" as advancing the likelihood that increasing numbers of people will regard themselves "as caretakers and/or equal parts of nature rather than dominators."[14]

Merchant proposes as exemplars of moral agency along these lines the Chipko women—the tree-hugging movement active in India in the 1970s and 1980s which resisted the incursions of lumbercutters and agents of "cash-cropping," forest-clearing agribusiness into groves which these women held sacred and integral to their indigenous economic life. These women's protests were nonviolent yet confrontational, involving song, marches, sign-carrying, and tree-hugging in the company of their children.[15] For Merchant, an adequate environmental ethic will be feminist, ecologically informed, historically aware, and resistant. It will also be appreciative of the local, the traditional, and the sacred.

Among ecofeminist writers, one who has contributed greatly to the reenvisioning of the sacrality of nature is theologian Sallie McFague.

McFague and the "Body of God" Metaphor

Metaphors and models and their use in theology have long been McFague's stock in trade. In an early work, she makes four points which seem key to understanding the later development of her ecofeminist thought.

First, she finds past notions of a "sacramental" universe untenable, despite the appeal of their organicism and their perception of the world's unity in God. McFague is concerned that "contemporary sensibility" is so marked by perceptions of fragmentation and disjunction that a cheerful "sacramental sensibility" with its underlying understanding of "the analogy of being by which all that is is because of its radical dependence on God" no longer has the capability of speaking to postmoderns.[16]

Second, since metaphors and models in religious expression have tended in the past to move from the suggestive and heuristic to the literalized and thus to become idols, there is a need, McFague believes, for new models and metaphors for depicting the God-world-human relation.[17]

Third, metaphors, and the models derived from them, illuminate similarities between things and sometimes help us grasp—even with startlement—what something is. Yet they always carry with them "similarity in the midst of dissimilars."[18] So metaphors and models have about them an "is/is not" quality.[19]

Fourth, McFague makes it clear that feminism, and thus ecofeminism, is a form of postmodernism. Therefore, it will find quite inadequate those models, axioms, and principles which smack of Enlightenment thought or are narrowly locked into male, Western, Judaeo-Christian experience.[20]

Suggesting that only a revisionist image of the universe as "sacramental" can speak—one that incorporates integration and disintegration, splendor and suffering, order and chaos—McFague proposes in *Models of God* that giving "the metaphor of the world as God's body a try" might be fruitful.[21] For McFague, this model, which she develops in *The Body of God,* imagines that planet and cosmos are where God is "embodied" or "bodied forth."[22] It has the advantage of implying that all components of creation are involved in the divine embodiment and thus have their own unique worth.

A number of assumptions underlie McFague's development of this model or metaphor. One, certainly, is that the ecofeminist attribution of ecological blame to a patriarchal, dualistic, hierarchical system of thought and to its allied technocratic, consumerist social order is correct. Another assumption is that the evolutionary, cosmological account of Earth origins which has developed in the last century and a half is an accurate and important grounding for understanding the organic interrelatedness of all beings. A third is that "the planetary agenda"—the call to human beings to reform environmental behaviors radically—is an urgent matter of justice. It is a matter which affects all beings, present and future, not only for the short term but, "as Native American traditions insist, 'for seven generations,' or for as long as we can imagine."[23] All of these, "the land and its creatures have rights and are intrinsically valuable."[24]

McFague is convinced that using the metaphor or model of the universe as "the body of God" can mutually assist theology and ecology and restore something of the lost sense of the sacred. As McFague sees it, the notion of divine transcendence is preserved but redefined in this model. Transcendence is understood as the vivifying spirit in the world, the life-giving force which brings things to life and motion.[25] It also preserves the notion of divine immanence by its panentheism. Furthermore, it extends the doctrine of incarnation beyond Jesus the Christ to a cosmic Christ, to the universe of beings which "incarnate" God in their own distinct ways. The ancient attribution of "omnipresence" to deity is retained in this model's depiction of God as all-present and everpresent in, through, and to creation.

The immediate ethical implication of Sallie McFague's model is that "bodies are important... and we ought to know and love them, our own and others."[26] What needs to be corrected, McFague believes, is the long tradition of love-hate, admiration-fear which has been directed toward the body and the physical world in Western Christian culture—a fierce ambivalence epitomized in the simultaneous "worship and loathing" of female bodies.[27] What needs to be asserted is the good of difference, multiplicity, even a certain bizarreness of bodies as an organic, cosmic, divine richness.[28] McFague calls bodies, including those most overlooked and neglected, "the primary context for obligation," and she describes a properly emergent environmental ethic as both "biocentric and cosmocentric."[29]

To assist the realization of such a "biocentric and cosmocentric" ethic, McFague recommends an "attention epistemology" marked by attentiveness and response to the other, awareness of the other as end-in-itself possessed of special worth. "Feminist epistemology" is a type of "attention epistemology" which is most adept at discerning "embodied differences" and prizing them, McFague believes.[30] This attentiveness and prizing of the diversity and goodness manifest in creation should evoke a "solidarity with all earth's creatures, especially the vulnerable," McFague declares.[31]

Practical eco-ethical conclusions which McFague draws from her "biocentric and cosmocentric" vision include the following:

1) Due to the finitude of planet Earth and in order to promote diversity and multiplicity, "population control and lifestyle changes" are imperative for humans.[32]

2) To effect positive change and life within appropriate limits, each individual must do his or her part in advancing the "planetary agenda," and groups at all socio-political levels must act collectively (and, insofar as possible, collegially) to reinvigorate the Earth.

3) Human beings have special obligations to the poor and oppressed. "Nature is, in our time," McFague urges, "the new poor"[33] and thus in need of reparative action, even while reconstruction and restitution on behalf of poor and oppressed humans are also pursued

McFague, like deep ecologists, resists being more specifically prescriptive about the intricate and interwoven environmental and societal issues which arise today. She is sure, however, that complex cases must be understood as embedded in a new matrix, a newly understood ecocosmic reality. Reliable judgments can be made only with careful examination of this matrix.

Sallie McFague's ecotheology and its corollary eco-ethics is perceived by her as one which "decenters and recenters human beings."[34] She makes it clear that humans are the loci of morality, and the human is highly responsible as knower and actor in the "planetary agenda." This "agenda," as she sees it, would improve the lot of the least advantaged humans and the most threatened species and ecosystems. It would construct a new "biocentric and cosmocentric" axiology as it displaces patriarchy. And it would do so within a Christian context wherein Christ is understood more cosmically, salvation is understood as "the good life" with maximal depth, breadth, and extent in this world, and where a cardinal sin is "ecological sin—wanting to have everything for oneself and one's kind."[35]

Ruether and the Gaia-God Connection

Another theologian at the forefront of ecofeminism is Rosemary Radford Ruether, editor of *Women Healing Earth* and author of what is already a kind of ecofeminist classic, *Gaia and God,* along with numerous articles and chapters on feminist and ecofeminist theology. Ruether offers, in *Gaia and God,* the observation that the core ambiguity of human nature—the capacity and drive for transcendence of "our mortal limits" and the fact that we are, as a species, merely one among the many "organisms that grow and then die"—provides the anthropological grounding for ethical interactions with the environment. The human capacity for transcendence carries with it a conscious capacity for "increased kindness," Ruether says. Therefore: "An ecological ethic must be based on acceptance of both sides of this dilemma of humanness, both the way we represent the growing edge of what is 'not yet' of greater awareness and benignity, and also our organic mortality, which we share with the plants and animals."[36]

Allied to the ambiguous position of the transcendence-driven yet mortal human is another ambiguity: the coexistence of the human impulse to the transformative improvement or "reshaping" of nature—an impulse which apparently is "natural" to humans and the situation of the "finite limits" of nature and all that lives in the natural world. Of this second ambiguity, Ruether remarks: "Ecological ethics is an uneasy synthesis of both these 'laws': the law of consciousness and kindness, which causes us to strain beyond what 'is,' and the laws of Gaia, which regulate what kinds of changes in 'nature' are sustainable in the life system of which we are an inextricable part."[37]

For Ruether, the key to living amidst these ambiguities and negotiating their perplexities with wisdom and grace requires the eschewing of systems of "domination" and the retrieval of a "sacramental" sense of the universe.[38] The perception of the Earth as Gaia, a living, energetic, creative system—indeed, an all-embracing organism (so named after the Earth goddess of the Greeks)—and the perception of Gaia as "matrix of life" can be formative, not of a spirituality of self-abnegation or ego-renunciation but, rather, of the merging of "small selves" and the "surrender" of self which Earth-healing requires.[39]

Like most ecofeminists, Ruether presumes that there is little need to be prescriptive in detail about appropriate eco-ethics so long as the vision is brought to clarity. The form which eco-ethical action takes will be the tangible manifestation of the vision. Opting for an organismic ecological vision does not preclude, however, naming what sorts of choices will be consistent with that vision and what sorts will be markedly inconsistent.

For Ruether, the notably inconsistent choices would be those marked by a patriarchal, dominating, dualistic, egotistically utilitarian mentality. Environmental "evil," says Ruether, "lies in the 'wrong' relationship."[40] Right relations—and these are covenantal—can be built if community bonds are "primary and regional,"smaller and more local, as deep ecology suggests. Right relations also presume a broad definition of "rights" such that human beings heed the "right of all members of the community to an equitable share in the means of subsistence." Finally, right relations call for a culture of "compassionate solidarity" rather than a cultural dynamic of supersedence-subservience and victor-vanquished such as is prevalent in patriarchy.[41]

When right relations prevail, certain choices would seem to be dictated by the bonds of relationship. Such choices would include, Ruether suggests: general technological and social restructuring; implementation of the use of "renewable energy sources"; improved mass transportation systems and residential/work site planning to avoid the necessity of long commutes; less energy-intensive and more efficient home heating and cooling systems; agricultural reform and more equitable food distribution; vastly decreased meat-eating; composting and recycling; human population decrease according to methods which are respectful of women and the poor; real "empowerment of women"; "genuine demilitarization"; consciousness-raising in local "biospheric communities."[42]

Like Tallmadge and various deep ecologists and like other spokespersons for ecofeminism, Ruether believes that appropriate eco-ethical behaviors must have a spiritual basis. Her ecofeminist spirituality embraces Gaia as living Earth, a God/dess who is both transcendent and immanent, an awakening divine force in a sacramental universe. This God/dess comes to multiform self-expression in the beings teeming within the local bioregion and landscape and within the human person's own being—a potentially growing, seed-planting, nurturing being.

In her introduction to the collection of ecofeminist writings by African, Asian, and Central and South American women, *Women Healing Earth,* Ruether highlights themes apparent in Sallie McFague's writings, the reflections of numerous other ecofeminists and her own: first, how the subjugation enforced by political or economic colonialism, "the domination of women," and "the domination of nature" are all tightly linked; secondly, how religion, often itself an agent of "such domination," can be reimaged, reclaimed, and renewed as "a resource for liberation from violence for both women and nature."[43]

Of high interest to Ruether is the way in which many native women seem to be unself-consciously ecofeminist (eco-mujerista, etc.), though there seems little likelihood that Chilean, Filipino, or Zimbabwean women would apply such appellations to themselves. She remarks on the phenomenon of "Northern ecofeminists" who "fail to make real connections between their own reality as privileged women and racism, classism, and impoverishment of nature."[44] What Ruether discovers is that, in the eyes of marginalized women, even militantly ecofeminist women, since they live lives of abundance, with no scarcity of comforts, cannot be spared indictment for many of the sins and crimes which they allege are the sins and crimes of patriarchy. Ruether's *Women Healing Earth* presents its various Third World reflections with a sting: an inevitable critique of First World ecofeminism.

A final observation should be made about Ruether's ecofeminism and religion. Ruether finds it of considerable significance that the Andean God is "as much mother as father...*Pachamama*"[45] and that an Asian woman like Sun Ai Lee-Park can read in the Bible "an ecotheology of liberation."[46] There is in Ruether a steady desire to retrieve what she regards as the best, the truest, and the most healthful of the Christian tradition but also to combine and redefine doctrine multiculturally and pluralistically. It is not surprising, then, that she applauds a blending of "Christian and indigenous African cosmology" such as seems to have occurred in some tribal cultures. She finds such a blending beneficial for a reconceiving of human-Christ-nature relations.[47]

As mentioned earlier, key to Ruether's ecofeminist reflections is the question of how to negotiate ambiguities. Among the resources for aiding that process, she finds the Earth wisdom of the Andean Pachamama and the Shona cosmological traditions. She also notes that the Christian Bible, despite accusations that it is insufferably steeped in patriarchal thought, can be read with a new hermeneutic and thus a new light in the Orient. For her, the restoration of a sense of the sacredness of the natural world depends on an amalgam of insights and impulses from the world's peoples and the world's religions.

A Note on Women Writers and Symbolizers

The priority which ecofeminism puts on the relational, the reflective, the spiritual, and the affective makes it no surprise that collections of somewhat more academic (and socially critical) essays will have in their midst not only contributions from indigenous peoples but also poetry, ritual, and drama expressive of a multiplicity of racial and ethnic perspectives. Rachel Bagby, for example, uses free verse and an extended dialogue with her African American mother as her "essay" on the environmental group called Philadelphia Community Rehabilitation Corporation, which her mother founded.[48] Carol Lee Sanchez uses a poem-proclamation, Native American story, and a blessing to tell of harmonious tribal ways.[49] Lina Gupta intersperses entries from her personal journal in an explication of Hindi beliefs about the Ganges river goddess Ganga.[50] It seems that ecofeminist writings cannot overly long sustain dispassionate, distanced intellectual exercises in environmental theory and ethical consideration. "Essays" which blend genres and allow the entry of personal experience, the pronoun "I," conversation, incantation, and felt memory bespeak something of the heart of ecofeminism: the belief that blending and border-crossing should proceed in women's ways.

Along with ecofeminist writing which uses song, symbol, ceremony, and human interchange, there is also a significant body of work which has contributed greatly to the projects of ecofeminism and environmental thought in general: nature writing by women. Without claiming (or meriting) the name "ecofeminist," Annie Dillard (who seems quite resolutely un-feminist in many ways) has piqued the natural imagination and is often cited for a type of nature mysticism in her works from *Pilgrim at Tinker Creek* on.[51] Literary biographer Linda Smith has found it possible to derive from Dillard ten "instructions" for creative spiritual living, at least half of which are ecospiritual.[52]

Aside from Dillard, a host of other women have contributed significant works that celebrate the attentiveness and sensitivity to nature which deep ecology, ecofeminism, and environmental holism in particular cherish. As works of encounter, they express relationality, majesty, and an awe that sometimes mixes wonder and terror. Stephanie Kaza, Gretel Ehrlich, Sue Hubbell, Kathleen Norris, Kathleen Dean Moore, and Marcia Bonta are among those who stimulate the natural imagination, summon memory, and evoke a sense of affinity with the natural world by their vibrantly descriptive writing and their insightful observations. Mary Austin's 1903 *Land of Little Rain* has attained a kind of contemporaneity with its 1988 reissuing.[53] These authors, among others, contribute observation and commentary, autobiography, stories of cities and plains, remembrances of treks along rivers and canyons. In their writing, societal structures and artifices, whether these authors regard them as "patriarchal" or not, fade as the elemental comes to the forefront. Birds, grasses, morning fogs, night smells, panoramic landscapes emerge as they are: life-shapers.

What Kind of Eco-Ethic?

Ecofeminism as a type of environmental ethics in some ways resists classification. It seems correct to say that it is a "visional" ethic wherein values and virtues arise inductively alongside a vision of the universe as an evolving process and the Earth as a living organism. It can also be said to be empirically based, grounded, as Rosemary Radford Ruether and Anne Clifford insist, on a sound scientific grasp of cosmos and ecology while also being intuitive in the sense that right judgments derive from what Nobel prize-winning scientist Barbara McClintock has called "a feeling for the organism."[54] Ecofeminism's insistence on the importance of the sense of the sacred also suggests an intuitive ethic.

Ecofeminism shares much of deep ecology's "ontology" in that it perceives the drive for fulfillment and flourishing, or "self-realization," as essential to being. It also subscribes to many of the norms of the "deontology" of the Naess-Sessions "platform"—biospheric or biocentric egalitarianism, non-hierarchicalism, an interest in the reversal of human population growth trends, and an emphasis on locale or bioregion as the center of ecological activity and decision-making. Ecofeminism seems, however, to be most aptly described as a teleological ethic. The goal or end of all living systems is seen to be harmonious, organic flourishing. Whatever advances this harmony and is beneficial to the well-being of each part of a living system is good. Whatever engenders disharmony, breakdown, and causes needless damage or death is bad.

An ecofeminist eco-ethic may be said to be biocentric and eco-centric. Envisioning all of what makes of the Earth the dynamic, living "Gaia" makes it biocentric and invites, as Rosemary Radford Ruether suggests, a "biophilic" response.[55] Cliffs, ice floes, and crystals are not regarded as nonliving. Holding that every unique part of the whole has "intrinsic value" and yet cannot be treated as separate from or unrelated to the whole makes an ecofeminist ethic ecocentric. Despite these characteristics, ecofeminism, because of its appeal for the feminization of consciousness, has, however, been imputed to be gynocentric and thus, perhaps unwittingly, anthropocentric.

The existence of a rift between ecofeminism and deep ecology has been highlighted by Ariel Salleh, Warwick Fox, Rosemary Radford Ruether, and Deborah Slicer, among others, in a discussion which has persisted for well over a decade. Michael Zimmerman has attempted a mediating position. Marti Kheel and Donald Davies, meanwhile, have championed a corrective one.

Ariel Salleh appears to have sparked the debate with a 1984 article in which she applauded many of the norms of deep ecology but critiqued what she regarded as its inattention to androcentrism and the perils of patriarchal thinking. She declared:

> [T]he deep ecology movement will not truly happen until men are brave enough to rediscover and to love the woman inside themselves. And we women, too, have to be allowed to love what we are, if we are to make a better world.[56]

Warwick Fox has responded to this call with the charge that the ecofeminist fixation on androcentrism as *"the* real root of ecological destruction" is "simplistic." He counters (and herein lies the incipient charge that ecofeminism is gynocentric):

> [I]t is actually perfectly possible to conceive of a society that is nonandrocentric, socioeconomically egalitarian, non-racist, and nonimperialist with respect to other human societies, but whose members nevertheless remain aggressively anthropocentric in collectively agreeing to exploit their environment for their collective benefit in ways that nonan-thropocentrists would find thoroughly objectionable.[57]

Fox, bypassing or discounting Salleh's assumption that the freeing of "the woman inside" would also liberate nature and creatures from domination and abuse, cites ecofeminists for a potentially harmful anthropocentrism of their own.

Fox's critique would seem to apply equally to Donald Davies' proposal for the reclaiming of "sophia" and for the establishment of "androgynous nonhierarchical thinking." Davies develops the notion that a "participatory, empathic, and often 'unconscious'" epistemology, which he terms "female," is the sure counter to the prospect of "repressive matriarchy."[58] He does not, however, make it entirely clear how a new "female" or a purposefully "androgynous" approach can be guaranteed to be "biocentric" or egalitarian. If the goal of the feminization of thinking and deliberating is gynocentrism or androgyny, why not a more inclusive (Fox calls it "transpersonal") transformation of consciousness—zoophilic, herbophilic, and geophilic, or "Gaian"—instead of a female-focused transformation?

Rosemary Radford Ruether has pointed out that the construction of matrifocal myths may be largely artifice and that the identification of women with nature can itself be "stereotypic."[59] Yet she notes that deep ecology too is prone to stereotyping and masculinizing. (It should perhaps be mentioned here that deep ecology anthologies are marked by a preponderance of contributions by male authors.) Speaking of EarthFirst! in particular (part of the deep ecology "movement"), Ruether observes:

> In contrast to ecofeminism, they stress anthropocentrism, rather than patriarchy, as the false thinking that underlies human destruction of "nature." Their preference for wilderness and an idealized hunting society as the "image" of the original harmony of humans and "nature" seems to reflect a masculine imagination quite different from the idea of the "good life" that appears in ecofeminism, where settled agricultural villages, domestic life, and the arts find a place.[60]

While Ruether herself would seem to be capable of being charged with some stereotyping too, by implying that women are collectively more sympathetic with domesticity and the arts, she attempts to avoid "essentialism"[61] and stridently condemns the "separatist vision of Mary Daly," who recommends the renunciation of male society and companionship altogether.[62] What Ruether seems to suggest is that the radical ecofeminism of Mary Daly and the masculinism of the deep ecology movement are equally undesirable. Ruether wants to see a certain gentling and feminization of eco-ethical attitudes and behaviors but also an integration of the human sexes with each other as well as with the nonhuman world.

Deborah Slicer believes that a great divide between ecofeminism and deep ecology exists largely because of misunderstanding and inattention. It exists, at least in its representation by Warwick Fox, because of a failure on the part of Fox to let ecofeminists speak for themselves. Slicer observes (correctly) that Fox's sources for ecofeminist theory are really secondary ones, Michael Zimmerman and Jim Cheney, rather than the women who themselves have developed ecofeminist thought and have observed its at-odds relations with deep ecology.[63] Slicer protests: "Ecofeminists do reject anthropocentrism, and soundly, for its own sake. However, their analyses of 'human-centeredness' in this culture are quite a bit more complex than the deep ecologists' analyses of it."[64]

Slicer finds that anthropocentrism in patriarchal cultures follows a notably dichotomizing and hierarchicalizing "logic." This "logic" is androcentric in such a way that sexism, classism, racism, and the denigration of nature run rampant under the dominating group.[65] Slicer concludes that a continuing problem may very well be an incompatibility between the understanding of the "self" which ecofeminists promote and the "expanded self" in deep ecology—an expansion which seems to her to diminish the significance of distinctions and simply to melt all lifeforms into one self-centered morass which may, in the end, be (as Val Plumwood has charged) "an enlargement and extension of egoism."[66] Distinctive to ecofeminism, says Slicer, is its promotion of "intraspecies egalitarianism along with interspecies egalitarianism."[67] For Slicer, the charge that ecofeminism is gynocentric would then be dismissable because she believes that ecofeminism champions a vision of relationality which deep ecology, particularly in Fox's "transpersonal" form, seems not to glimpse.

Michael Zimmerman's attempt at mediation rests on the conviction that both ecofeminism and deep ecology desire a similar Earth-healing and the demise of many of the same destructive socio-cultural patterns and practices. Both diagnose, Zimmerman says, "the illness of Western culture."[68] Zimmerman agrees that "[w]omen and men alike have been distorted by the effects of patriarchy" and that a part of what is needful is a recovery of the sacred. Zimmerman concedes: "Perhaps...a postpatriarchal God/dess is necessary for women and men alike to develop a form of individuation that does not involve dissociation from the body, from nature, and from woman."[69]

What Zimmerman sees as possibly emergent is an ethic of care that is all-embracing. Zimmerman, then, in noting the traces of syncretism in deep ecology and ecofeminism, would not see any point to their volleying charges back and forth. Rather like Naess, who sees all manner of ecosophies as viable, Zimmerman would judge ecofeminism and deep ecology basically compatible. What remains problematic, however, is that by simply acknowledging patriarchal damages and then recommending that the two schools proceed with their "common search,"[70] Zimmerman too may be vulnerable to accusations that his awareness of androcentrism is merely superficial and thus his analysis of the sources of eco-ethical problems is too shallow.

Such would seem to be a conclusion derivable from Marti Kheel. Her psycho-literary analysis of passages from deep ecologists about "widened identification" and the hunt points to a profound opposition between the aggressive features of "male" imagination and the protective features of "female" imagination and "identification."[71] For Kheel, there are psychosexual issues that need much more penetrating analysis, and there are dangers inherent in a kind of "holism" that obliterates the individual and "particular."[72] Like Zimmerman, Kheel would find gynocentrism absent from ecofeminism. Unlike him, she suggests that there are perceptible unresolved issues in deep ecological thinking which remain a barrier to a working merger between deep ecology and ecofeminism.

From the ecofeminist viewpoint, then, their own school of ecophilosophical, ecotheological, and eco-ethical thought has unique insights and unique analyses to present. Ecofeminism's wide-ranging concerns include nature, marginalized peoples, social and cultural systems, structures of thinking, and the well-being of all that lives. Numerous ecofeminists have also remarked upon, while others have written at length on, the treatment of animals.[73] An insistent point made by ecofeminists is, however, that an ethic of "obligations and rights" is not adequate for addressing the concerns of animals.[74] Such a claim puts ecofeminism at odds in principle, though not in conclusions, with much of the thinking represented in the next chapter, where "animal rights" are discussed.

3
Animal "Rights" and
Questions of Human Behavior

When the introductory reader *Ethics* appeared in 1994, editor Peter Singer included among its five sections one entitled "Common Themes in Primate Ethics." In the section "codes" for behavior concerning familial relations, interpersonal (or inter-chimpanzee) reciprocity, and sexual expression are explored. Tribal peoples, ancient Jews and Babylonians, twentieth-century men at war, and nonhuman primates are the subjects of the section's twelve articles. Appearing among these studies of "primate ethics" are Jane Goodall's "Helping Kin in Chimpanzees" and "Incest Avoidance Among Chimpanzees," Frans de Waal's "Chimpanzee Justice" and "The Rules of Chimpanzee Sex," and Robert Trivers' "The Evolution of Reciprocal Altruism" (which includes a consideration of practices among "early hominids").[1]

In his introduction to the text, Singer makes clear his own conviction that "human ethics evolved from the social instincts that we inherited from our non-human ancestors." He critiques Kant's insistence that reason (as measured by humans) is the basis for moral duty and proposes that a Humean view of ethics as having a more emotional, passionate base is preferable. For Singer, certain types of "ethical" behavior can be detected among such primates as chimpanzees and gorillas, and this challenges any and all who would decline to give them (or other higher functioning animals) moral status. Singer has elsewhere set forth his position that neither "all lives" nor even all primate lives are equivalent but that "where animals and humans have similar interests...those interests are to be counted equally, with no automatic discount just because one of the beings is not human."[2]

With American ethicist Tom Regan, Australian Singer is at the forefront of an "animal liberation" or "animal rights" movement in ethics. It is a movement which claims some origin in the thought of utilitarian Jeremy Bentham, who is frequently cited for his proposal that the capacity for suffering rather than for reasoning or talking ought to be the starting point for discussion of "moral status" and the recipients of humanity's "moral duties."[3]

Like ecofeminism, "animal rights" thinking rejects dualistic, mechanistic Cartesian thought as unwonted in its effects on Western behavior and unwarranted in light of the evidence of non-"mechanical" behavior and phenomena exhibited in the nonhuman world, particularly in the lives of "some animals."[4] Empirical observations of awareness, feeling, preferences, and the pursuit of certain "interests" on the part of animals laid the groundwork for much of the "animal rights" movement in ethics. Thus, side by side with evaluations of the regard or nonregard for animals found in the philosophical tradition (with Aristotle, Aquinas, Montaigne, Spinoza, Descartes, Hume, Kant, and Bentham often commented on, pro and con), the reader of "animal rights" ethicists finds citations of environmental writers like Aldo Leopold (treated in Chapter 4) and Barry Lopez.[5]

Fundamental to "animal rights" or "animal liberation" thinking are several premises: that "higher" animals (primates at least and perhaps all mammals, though Singer also seems to include fish and fowl) "have beliefs and desires"; that they can be said to "retain a psychophysical identity over time"; and that they "have a kind of autonomy—preference autonomy." These qualities qualify animals for status as "moral patients" and lead "rights" or "liberation" ethicists to judge that animals enjoy "the basic moral right to respectful treatment" and that human moral agents have a "prima facie duty not to harm" animals.[6]

Whether the ethicist takes the "preference utilitarian" path of Singer or the more deontological path of egalitarian justice theory found in Regan, the conclusions seem to be that animals have an inherent right to be respected by humans, that certain things are "due" them, and that there is a presumption against killing or causing them needless pain, based on human "duty not to harm" any individual "subject-of-a-life."[7] For Singer, such thinking results in a moral prohibition of meat-eating and an insistence on the obligation of vegetarianism. For Regan, it leads to condemnation of "animal agriculture," hunting, trapping, and experimentation and testing on animals in educational programs, cosmetic trials, and scientific research.[8] Not all "rights" thinkers, however, are quite so strong on "intrinsic value" or "inherent rights" questions, nor are they quite so definite about prohibitions.

Taking a rather different tack, Anthony Povilitis argues that "rights" are "intrinsic" only in "an intuitive, or...a mystical sense." They "cannot belong to the essential nature or constitution of a thing" and thus can only be "assigned." Rights are not quantifiable, demonstrable, or constitutive. The "assignment" or attribution of rights to beings is "a function of...perceived value" in those beings, says Povilitis. Humans, who function as perceivers of value and as agents capable of protecting value, accord rights to other humans because they value humanity in general. Povilitis argues that there is no good reason for declining to extend rights farther, since there can be new or remediated perceptions of value, and, as far as he is concerned, the ability to talk back or to return valuation has nothing to do with the "assignment" of rights.[9] Povilitis goes on to comment that it is altogether proper to speak of certain "primary" rights of living things and of nature—namely, to exist and to be free from "unnecessary suffering." Without worrying over the semantic or behavioral concerns in Singer and Regan, who take pains to redefine terms and to renounce certain traditions, Povilitis objects that those who deny "rights" to nonhumans and quibble over questions of moral status, requirements of moral agency, and reciprocity are "excessively anthropocentric" in their approach. It seems that for Povilitis a new worldview, or at least a new view of inter-animal relations, not only allows for but invites a new understanding of the extent of "rights" and of who or what might be rights holders.

"Speciesism"

From the mid-1970s on, Singer, Regan, and other like-minded thinkers have routinely identified a deep-seated "speciesism" like that implied by Povilitis as the root of erroneous Western attitudes and behaviors toward nonhumans.[10] Like racism or sexism, "speciesism" is seen as an ill-founded belief in the superiority of a group, in this case the species *homo sapiens,* which is used as a justification for the mistreatment and misuse of those outside the group, in this case nonhumans. It seems that "speciesism" as a prejudice is equivalent to anthropocentrism as a mindset.

Regan holds that there ought to be a basic egalitarianism of moral status and moral interests among species. (He seems to mean among animal species.) Regan allows for the possibility that a member of any species might forfeit its right not to be harmed or caused pain. A human may still kill a rabid dog to save his or her own human child from attack without being deemed "speciesist," Regan implies. The rationale for this allowance is that degrees and gravity of harms differ and that harm threatened to a greater *number* of individuals can be the deciding factor. Here the decision is in favor of saving the child *not* because it is a human but because the number of other individuals likely to be affected and the degree of effect likely from the death of the child tend to "override" the "rights" of the dog. The reader of Regan has to presume that Regan avoids getting into arguments over whether rabid dogs must be considered unjust aggressors (as attacking humans would be considered when they forfeit their rights to be spared harm) by invoking his "minimize harm" principle.[11]

Despite his disclaimers, Regan's position seems to be a utilitarian one. The deontological principle of protection of innocent life (the attacked child's) is preserved, but considerable weight is given to multiple effects and even side effects of an anticipated action. The reader of Regan has to imagine that the calculus of the decision in favor of the child takes into account not only the painful (or deadly) outcome for the child but also the grief or deprivation caused to the child's parents, grandparents, friends, playmates, even the backyard birds it feeds. The harm done to the dog may be fatal, but it appears to be experienced only by the dog and its possible owners. Its canine relatives are presumably not capable of grieving—though one cannot be sure.[12] In any case, Regan would suggest that initially both child and dog have equal rights to live and not to be harmed. Where a choice between lives and/or harms must be made, the nonspeciesist solution includes an assessment of a variety of factors and must conclude that a particular choice presents itself as causing less harm than the alternative choice does.

In a 1990s treatment of the topic of "speciesism," Regan defines what he calls "categorical speciesism." He declares:

> [I]t is the belief that (1) the inherent value of an individual
> can be judged solely on the basis of the biological species to
> which that individual belongs, and that (2) all the members
> of species Homo sapiens have equal inherent value, while
> all the members of every other species lack this kind of
> value, simply because all and only humans are members of
> the species Homo sapiens.[13]

What Regan has consistently resisted in his writings is giving priority to human interests. He urges that animals possessed of sentience be regarded as having an "inherent value" which demands the kind of equality of regard or moral consideration usually thought, in democratic societies, to be reserved to human citizens. It must be added that, while Regan usually generalizes about "animals," it seems that planaria, nematodes, locusts, and mosquitoes do not hold "rights" and do not qualify as "subjects-of-a-life." Being a "subject-of-a-life" requires some level of awareness, some capacity to express preferences, and detectable movement toward apparent goals. In Regan, however, the division between "subjects-of-a-life" and nonsubjects is not altogether clear. What is clear is that the margin between rights holding and rights lacking is not drawn at the borders of species *homo sapiens.*

An approach to questions of animal ethics which emphasizes human kinship with many other animal species can also be found in moral philosophers James Rachels and Mary Midgley. Rachels does not hold forth about "speciesism," but he proposes that a perception of the inherent worth of humanity's animal kin should underlie the "moral individualism" he proposes as a replacement for "human dignity" ethics. Rachels' "moral individualism" suggests a regard for animals on their own terms. Human interests and desires are not preferred, yet there is not a pure egalitarianism. Rachels suggests that "our treatment of individual creatures…should be adjusted to fit the actual characteristics of those creatures."[14] For him, such an approach raises serious questions about humans' killing of animals and their inflicting pain on them in slaughtering, cosmetic production, and scientific research. Rachels' own tendencies, though he does not absolutize them, are to conclude that "killing an animal that has a rich biographical life might be more objectionable than killing one that has a simpler life," that many cosmetic and scientific practices ought to be suspended, and that vegetarianism may turn out to be a virtually exceptionless norm.[15]

Mary Midgley, in works like *Beast and Man* and *Animals and Why They Matter,* lays philosophical and scientific foundations for regarding animals as ends in themselves and for shifting to a philosophical anthropology which helps humanity to see itself as "part of a whole much greater than [it]self, one in which other members excel [the human] in innumerable ways."[16] She argues that there is a continuum of animalkind-humankind which must be acknowledged and honored, despite disputations against animal-human likeness in much of the philosophical tradition. Midgley disdains egalitarian language and the term "speciesism," however, and prefers to speak of breaking "the species barrier."[17] Breaking the "barrier" invites greater respect for animals; avoiding egalitarian motifs and "rights" language allows, she believes, the acknowledgment of important individual and inter-specific differences. While she does not espouse particular causes like vegetarianism, hunting bans, etc., Midgley proposes reasons for crediting animals with "consciousness," feelings, various "subjective" behaviors and attributes, and she presses for an ethic in regard to animals that goes beyond "minimalism." At its heart, Midgley's argument is that "the species barrier" should be broken in such a way that animals are regarded as morally considerable and as entitled to making certain "claims" on humans,[18] though these claims cannot be verbal or juridical.

Both Midgley and Rachels are far from the position which Regan calls categorically "speciesist," and yet they do insist on taking into account differences—individual differences and inter-specific differences. Both conclude that humans have duties toward animals and that animals cannot be treated as mere manipulable things. Both too have an interest in overcoming what they perceive as biases in traditional Western thought which have contributed to an indifference toward animal suffering.

Jay McDaniel, who equates "speciesism" with "homocentrism," promotes a similarly "relational" point of view which eliminates "we" vs. "they" thinking and attributes intrinsic value to nonhuman beings.[19] He is among those who reach conclusions very like those of Regan and Singer without using "rights" language. Like Midgley and Rachels, McDaniel objects to the treatment of animals as "means to ends." Unlike Midgley, who makes no prescriptions and offers no definite proscriptions, McDaniel challenges common practices in livestock raising and chicken farming, policies of cosmetic testing, habits of fur-wearing and sport hunting, and "the exploitation of animals in recreation."[20] McDaniel is among those who promote an ethic of "respect" for animals while avoiding disputes over whether or not animals can be bearers of rights. He does not conclude, as Rachels seems to, that vegetarianism is a moral demand, but he suggests that for a variety of reasons—including concern for the world's poor and for the good of ecosystems—inhabitants of affluent societies "ought to reduce our consumption of meat and dairy products as much as possible."[21] A difference between McDaniel's approach and that of Singer, Regan, Rachels, and Midgley is that, while they frame their discussions in the language and concepts of philosophical ethics, he frames his more in the themes and tenets of a theology of creation and what has come to be known as "ecospirituality." McDaniel writes as a Christian who believes that God has made a "covenant with animals," loves them, and charges humans to do the same.[22] Like many who subscribe to an expandable liberation theology, McDaniel appears to accept the linkage of "speciesism" with racism, sexism, and other prejudices which ought to be overcome.

In Support of "Speciesism"

The concept of "speciesism," with its consequent condemnation by "animal rights," "animal liberation," and some "animal respect" thinkers, is understandably refuted by any system of thought which maintains that the human is unique, incomparable as a species, set apart in the powers of reason and linguistic articulation, and therefore possessed of rights, privileges, and powers which other beings cannot hold or approximate. Such an anthropocentric position can be maintained on philosophical grounds and can be held even by those who favor some sort of respectful attitude toward animals.[23] Or such a position can be defended by those who adopt a more laissez-faire attitude and believe that things as they are, even environmentally, fall within the natural and corrigible, and ought to remain subject to human direction and intervention without drastic changes in culture and mores.[24].

Despite the persistence of non-"green" politics and despite the resistance to "animal rights" thinking, religious ethicists and theologians would likely be as loath to proclaim "speciesism" laudable as they would be to suggest that racism or sexism is praiseworthy. Charles Pinches, however, in *Good News for Animals,* makes a cogent argument for a kind of "theological speciesism."

Pinches perceives in the "anthropocentric/nonanthropocentric distinction" a radical disjunction which in effect reinforces the notion that the welfare and interests of nonhumans are their own but "[have] nothing to do with my own."[25] Pinches suggests that human actions on behalf of humans must be understood in some sense as "anthropocentric" but cannot, merely on that basis, be deemed wrong or mal-centered. For Pinches, anthropocentrism (if understood as human focus on and preference for the well-being of humans) is not necessarily criminal, ethically disordered, or sinful, as "nonanthropocentric" thinkers can sometimes make it sound. What he proposes as an alternative to "nonanthropocentric" thought is an emphasis on "the integrity of creation" (a term adopted by the World Council of Churches; cf. Chapter 6) *if* this is understood not to be a collectivist "environmental holism" but as a concern for "the goodness of each of the parts" of the created world. Pinches terms this insistence "that each part of creation is good in and of itself as well as for others and God" a kind of "speciesism," but not a narrow, prejudicial one.[26]

Pinches calls his focus "theological speciesism," describing it as: moral concern for the well-being of whole species as well as for the individual members of species; attention not only to sentience and suffering but also to animals' "social" needs; consideration of plant species and efforts on behalf of endangered species, whether fauna or flora; grave moral questioning of humanity's attempts at "creation of new species," the "genetic manipulation" of species or some of their members, and the "domestication" of species or members of them.[27] Pinches also suggests that if humans take seriously the "naming function" given them in Genesis, they might well take into their care only as many creatures as they can name[28] and thus establish some level of rapport and relationship with them. Without getting into disputes about "egalitarian" policies, "rights," or "liberation," Pinches presents an ethic which calls for respect for animals, nonanimal life, and ecosystems. Pinches recommends that members of *homo sapiens* affirm that humans do have, and ought to exercise well, a "unique human role"— namely, that of "caretaker of diversity" on God's Earth.[29]

An affirmation of such a caretaking role calls for certain reforms in human behavior—including careful study of animal species as an aid to determine what sorts of behaviors may be right or wrong in regard to individual animals; concern for systems, species, and subspecies; special consideration for members of endangered species; cautions about practices connected with domestication and human use.[30] Pinches does not offer wholesale condemnations of meat-eating, hunting, keeping pets, or various instrumental uses of animals, but he does urge greater care about the impact on individual animals of certain actions and the effects on larger wholes of human practice vis-à-vis members of various species. Since the human remains the privileged determiner of what is right and wrong in regard to nonhuman life, and since the human has the obligation to grasp the outcomes of human behaviors (including killing, harming, causing pain, and using), Pinches' brand of "speciesism" might be called not so much anthropocentric as anthroporesponsible. It is a mixed individualist and holist ethic.

The Pinches article demonstrates the increasing tendency among environmental ethicists and ecotheologians to develop an "ethic of respect" that attends to the plight of animals and calls into question certain current practices, even if this ethic is developed as a kind of counteraction to "animal rights" thinking. Among the results of the "animal rights" or "animal liberation" movement in ethics is not only the politicization of the movement but also the imperative it has put upon ethical thinkers of a variety of philosophical and theological persuasions to respond to the contemporary situations in which animals are raised, used, and killed by humans.

"Speciesism" has, to date, neither been renounced nor expunged from ethical vocabulary. Whether or not it is a useful term, it has occasioned abundant discussion and a movement toward an ethical consensus that at least some fairly common human practices in regard to animals demand reconsideration.

A Review of Ethical Themes in "Animal Rights" Thinking

If one can give a name to the approach of adamant "animal liberation" or "animal rights" thinkers, it might well be "zoocentric," though a strong qualification immediately has to be made. The focus of ethicists of the Singer-Regan school is on animals possessed of sentience, animals which can register some level of pleasure or pain. On the margins of concern are apparently nonsentient animals, which may require some respect or consideration but do not have "rights" or need "liberation." For this reason, one would have to say that, despite talk about egalitarian interests and nonpreferential regard, there is a type of hierarchicalism in "animal rights" thought. Lower animals and plants are not "subjects-of-a-life" and therefore do not merit the ethical attention which sentient animal species do. The central moral dictum of "animal rights" and "animal liberation" ethics is that needless suffering in the lives of feeling animals ought to be prevented. The same can be said to be true of "animal respect" ethicists like Rachels, Midgley, McDaniel, and even Pinches. For some of these, the requirement of vegetarianism is a moral absolute; for others, like Regan, it is a norm which allows for occasional exception (such as in native cultures where food-gathering prospects are very constrained, as with Arctic Eskimos).[31] Others who allow meat-eating would enforce strict laws about conditions of livestock raising and slaughter. Some "animal rights" ethicists would undertake active and even heroic measures to rescue threatened animals, deliver antibiotics to herds suffering epidemics, and the like. Others would be more inclined to allow "nature" to take its course—unless the problems of illnesses were somehow human induced.

Often pointed out in criticism of "animal rights" thinking is that it is unflinchingly individualistic. Regan himself has admitted that species and systems are not covered by a "rights view," though "animal rights" thinkers would be expected to support sound environmental efforts and moves toward the preservation of species.[32] Well-functioning systems are clearly important, but it seems reasonable to conjecture that part of the reason why "animal rights" thinkers may be wary of speaking of the "rights" of systems or whole species is not merely because it is difficult to identify such wholes as "subjects-of-a-life." It is also perhaps because systems, wholes, collectivities may be found to function fairly well even if acts of cruelty and violence are meted out on some individual members. The *future*-concerns of this school of thought are focused more on the lifespans and quality of life of present, living animals; of notably less concern are their potential descendants or "future generations" of their species at large.

Aside from the well publicized opposition of much of the "animal rights" movement to meat-eating, fur-wearing, and hunting, a big issue for "animal rights" ethicists, and for many "animal respect" ethicists, is the use of animals in scientific research and cosmetic testing. Some (Regan, e.g.) would outright prohibit the use of animals in these programs. Others would seek alternatives and seriously limit the use of animals in scientific endeavors. For some, a criterion for the use of animals in experiments would be the potential helpfulness to the animal which might be gained by participation. In all cases of discussion of these matters (with the exception of discussion by those who are morally indifferent to the manner in which animals are used), it seems that actions which partake of cruelty, infliction of nontherapeutic pain, the creation of artificial living conditions and deprivations for the mere sake of scientific curiosity, are taboo.

In the "animal rights" school of thought, and in much of the "animal respect" writing, animals (sentient ones, at least) are regarded as morally considerable, have moral status, are clearly "moral patients." An occasional argument appears that certain animals have qualities and exhibit behaviors which constitute or approximate moral agency (as, for example, when monkeys decline to inflict pain on other monkeys in experimental situations even when they might be rewarded for causing pain).[33] Overall, "animal rights" and "animal liberation" thinking prescribes benign and benevolent coexistence on the part of humans with animals, a live-and-let-live attitude which minimizes humans' "use" of animals as if they were mere instruments, tools, things. Animals are perceived as having "intrinsic value," "inherent worth"—lives of their own which have meaning apart from human connections.

Toward Environmental Holism

Environmental holists, considered in the next chapter, are sometimes charged with indifference to individual creatures' well-being as they pursue their concern for well-functioning ecosystems and attend to the whole biosphere. Their ethic is found wanting if it presents an "integrity" of the natural world which still allows tangential or nonessential species to be sacrificed or trivializes the question of rightful treatment of individual animals.

"Animal liberation" and "animal rights" ethicists, on the other hand, are sometimes charged with having an "atomistic," "individualistic" preoccupation which ignores ethical issues pertaining to plant life, bioregions like rain forests, and even planetary well-being. As a result, some ethicists (like Laura Westra) have sought to develop a "joint ethic" which inculcates a "respect" for animals and yet allows for certain uses (some meat-eating, some scientific research) and admits that some "hostilities" between species in their pursuit of survival are inevitable and consonant with what is environmentally sound and "natural."[34] Such would seem to be the legacy of Aldo Leopold, a kind of progenitor of what is called, in the next chapter, the "naturalist" school. Leopold held a strong respect for wolves, deer, Wisconsin birds, lake and desert creatures, even while he continued to hunt and fish in careful, restrained ways. Solutions like Westra's (or Leopold's, for that matter) will likely remain unacceptable to "animal rights" activists and ethicists. And debate about who or what may hold "rights" appears to be doomed to perpetuity.

Despite what can be construed as vehement and occasionally vitriolic dispute about the moral status of animals and the rightful human treatment of them, it has to be acknowledged that the "animal rights" controversy has raised consciousness and prompted much ethical reflection.

The political effects have been felt in the English-speaking world, in Europe,[35] and in Africa (particularly in Kenya, where "shoot-to-kill orders" have been issued against elephant poachers).[36] Religious leaders and philosophical ethicists have been compelled to turn their attention to the treatment of animals. This is reflected in the way in which animals get special mention in the recent *Catechism of the Catholic Church,* in statements prepared for gatherings of the World Council of Churches, and in the *Global Ethic* presented by the Parliament of the World's Religions. British theologian Andrew Linzey has been named chaplain of the U.S. Humane Society by virtue of his writing and teaching on animal rights and his extensive work on a revisionist christology, anthropology, and liberation theology which accommodate animal rights thought.[37] Ecocentrist Holmes Rolston attends to "duties" toward animals. Deep ecologists and ecofeminists locate the origins of animal abuse in flawed hierarchical, anthropocentric and/or androcentric thinking. And liberation theologians note the costs to indigenous peoples and to rain forests when cattle-raising proceeds purely for profit. The exploitation of animals, land, and peoples seems inextricably linked.

What seems to be evolving in environmental ethical thought is a noteworthy attentiveness to animals and a fair level of consensus about their moral considerability. Some of this has come from a heightened awareness of human kinship and a more painstaking education about animals' habits and capacities. Promotion of "animal rights" as an ethical agenda continues to be a minority movement, but reflection on an ethic of respect for animals seems remarkably widespread. A Schweitzerian "reverence for life" which spares even insects is hardly popular, but there seems to be abroad a concession among philosophical and religious ethicists that human beings have often been remiss in their treatment of animals and that there is need for a new ethic of care, particularly for those who are closely related to human moral agents.

But, as Mary Midgley has observed, there are not only "social" claims made upon humans by conscious creatures but also "ecological" claims made by flora, landforms, and systems.[38] Approaches which attempt to take both into account and to balance the claims have been considered in previous chapters and are considered in the remaining chapters of this book.

4
The "Naturalists" and Leopoldian Ethics

At quite a remove from animal rights thinkers, whose focus is on the well-being of individual animals, are a multitude of holistic, ecocentric environmental philosophers and ethicists who are grouped together here as the "naturalist" school. All of these to some degree lay foundations for their thought in the work of Aldo Leopold, a 1906–1909 student of Yale's forestry program who enjoyed a long career in wildlife management, wildlands protection, university teaching, and writing until his death in 1948.

Susan Flader, J. Baird Callicott, Lawrence E. Johnson, Alan Miller, Robert Fuller, Peter Wenz, Roderick Nash, Van Rensselaer Potter, and Holmes Rolston III are among those who exhibit the influence of Leopold's "land ethic." Such themes as ecosystemic interdependence, reverence for all creation, the perception of the interactive mix of intrinsic and instrumental values in nonhuman beings, an active pro-biodiversity stance, a broad extension of "moral considerability," a commitment to sustainable living, a concern for Earth-restoration, a pursuit of the "natural," and an esteem for the "wild" mark the ethical reflections of these writers.

The Leopold Legacy

In her study of Leopold, *Thinking Like a Mountain,* Susan Flader shows that Leopold, a keen observer of natural processes, went through a number of transformations in his own perceptions. It was only after his own policies of "varmint" extermination had contributed to a population explosion among deer and an alteration in the brush and vegetation of the American Southwest that Leopold recognized the importance of predators like wolves and mountain lions to the stability which he had worked so hard to protect. By the 1930s, when he published his classic *Game Management* textbook and produced an essay called "A Biotic View of the Land," Leopold had developed an intricate understanding of the "definite relationships between the complex structure and the smooth functioning of the whole—between the evolution of ecological diversity and the capacity of the land organism for self-renewal, which he termed *stability* or *land health.*"[1]

The movement in Leopold's thought toward a wide concept of sustainability can be traced from earlier essays to the still much-quoted work which was completed just before his death, *A Sand County Almanac.* In one of his earliest writings, a letter to foresters in the Carson National Forest in New Mexico, Leopold, their young supervisor, urges them to judge policies and the enforcement of them according to the observable, comprehensive "effect on the forest."[2] In the early 1920s, in an essay entitled "Conservation in the Southwest," he begins speaking of nature as "a living thing" and calling for attentiveness to the "interdependent functions" of Earth elements. He encourages not only a practical scientific appreciation for diversity and complexity but also a religious one, remarking that since "God started his show a good million years before he had any men for an audience...it is just barely possible that God himself likes to hear birds sing and see flowers grow."[3] This is one of the relatively few religious references in Leopold's work.

In 1933, in "The Conservation Ethic," Leopold supports a kind of affirmative action on the part of landholders to expand the populations of "any wild plant, fish, bird or mammal" which can flourish on their properties by the conscious exertion of "building it a habitat." Leopold advocates here "a creative art of land-beauty which is the prerogative, not of esthetic priests but of dirt farmers, which deals not with plants but with biota."[4] For Aldo Leopold, foresters and wildlife managers and farmers are all seen as charged with a wide-ranging mandate to preserve not only the species which are their special interests (trees for lumbering, game for hunting, fish for fishing, crops for harvesting) but the whole host of interrelated species which can and should live in local ecosystems.

In 1939, in "A Biotic View of Land," Leopold pronounces the judgment which developed in the next decade into his larger "land ethic." He writes:

> Land, then, is not merely soil; it is a fountain of energy flowing through a circuit of soils, plants, and animals. Food chains are the living channels which conduct energy upward; death and decay return it to the soil. The circuit is not closed; some energy is dissipated in decay, some is added by absorption, some is stored in soils, peats, and forests, but it is a sustained circuit, like a slowly augmented revolving fund of life.[5]

Leopold cautions that the "biotic pyramid," the upflow of energy from land to more complex, living organisms, can be sustained only by human cooperation and human attentiveness to wise and moderate use of resources. He adds: "The combined evidence of history and ecology seems to support one general deduction: the less violent the man-made changes, the greater the probability of successful readjustment in the pyramid." One of the key factors in this "readjustment" is human population and its concentration, since "a dense population requires a more violent conversion of land."[6] With this remark Leopold becomes one of the earliest to enunciate a correlation between ecosystem functioning, prudential use, and temperate population patterns.

By the 1940s Leopold is found speaking of the land as a "community to which we belong," a community which humans must learn "to use...with love and respect."[7] In a lament over the passing of the last passenger pigeon, Leopold reflects:

> We know now what was unknown to all the preceding caravan of generations: that men are only fellow-voyagers with other creatures in the odyssey of evolution. This new knowledge should have given us, by this time, a sense of kinship with fellow-creatures; a wish to live and let live; a sense of wonder over the magnitude and duration of the biotic enterprise.[8]

The impress of observations over the years deepened in Leopold the conviction that sustenance and sustainability must be deliberate human choices, matters of policy. Without such choices, depletion and extinction of species and resources must ensue. Leopold declares the necessity for the development of "an ecological conscience" and notes that the well-being of the whole biotic community depends on it. "Health is the capacity of the land for self-renewal," says Leopold,[9] providing what might be the shortest and simplest definition of what the more recent "sustainability" movement is all about: protecting and preserving the capacity for "self-renewal" among species and resources.

The "land ethic" which Leopold proposes is largely a matter of vision and attitude. It requires a systems view, a sense of community which embraces "soils, waters, plants, and animals," a society in which the human is not "conqueror" but simply, says Leopold, a "plain member and citizen."[10] The human as a citizen who governs must accept the task, as Leopold sees it, of facilitating the functioning of the "biotic pyramid" or "land pyramid." The principle for a beneficial and beneficent "land ethic" can be stated quite briefly. "Examine each question in terms of what is ethically and esthetically right, as well as what is economically expedient," advises Leopold. "A thing is right when it tends to preserve the integrity, stability, and beauty of the biotic community. It is wrong when it tends otherwise."[11] This statement is the keystone, a kind of first great commandment, of Leopoldian ethics.

"Naturalists," Ecocentrists, and Leopoldian Variations

"That land is a community is the basic concept of ecology," observes Leopold in *A Sand County Almanac,* "but that land is to be loved and respected is an extension of ethics."[12] A number of environmental ethical writers have elaborated on the "extension of ethics" which Leopold envisioned. And a few, identifying themselves as inheritors of the Leopold tradition, have perhaps extended Leopold's thought beyond any "extension" he might have imagined.

Susan Flader and J. Baird Callicott have been promoters, editors, and explicators of Leopold's work. Flader has been more occupied with following Leopold's development and the refinement of his thought. Callicott has written of Leopold descriptively, but he also reads a number of prescriptions in him. Callicott, for example, labels Leopold's ethical method "deontological" since it emphasizes intrinsic goods, the intrinsically right, and human duties on behalf of the biotic community.[13] He indicates that Leopold's "energy circuit model of the environment" implies human moral obligations to protect endangered species, to exercise great care in any human-engineered change to ecosystems and habitats, and to preserve natural predators.[14] Callicott also takes considerable pains to emphasize the humanitarian and culture-appreciative notes in Leopold's writings. For Callicott it is clear that ethical preference, in hard cases, is given to "the inner social circles to which we belong" and that nonhumans are regarded as worthy of "respect" but not assigned anything comparable to "human rights."[15] Callicott is emphatic that "biocentric egalitarianism" such as is found in deep ecology is not Leopoldian, and the ecocentrism of the "land ethic" still allows primacy of moral consideration for fellow humans beings.

Callicott goes beyond the "land ethic" to describe what he calls "Leopold's Land Aesthetic." Such an aesthetic, informed by a knowledge of ecology and "evolutionary biology," enlarges the human capacity for cherishing prairies and swamps, sandhill cranes and alligators.[16] Leopold's "land aesthetic" would not only support national parks and protected wildernesses but would also offer private landowners ethical motivation for reforesting, wildflower seed scattering, chemical fertilizer-free vegetable gardens, and small habitat restoration. Callicott's reading of Leopold, certainly grounded in his declarations and anecdotes, seems a reasonable extension of Leopold's thought even while it becomes, for Callicott, a specific indicator that all sorts of things—from food preservatives through golf courses to Disney World—might have something ethically objectionable about them.

Another ecocentric philosopher of note is Lawrence E. Johnson, whose ethical stance is described by him as environmental "holism."[17] In his articles and his book, *A Morally Deep World*, Johnson's declared purpose is to avoid what he perceives as a faulty anthropocentrism and individualism in some strains of eco-ethical discussion. Johnson, drawing upon Leopold, urges that environmental thought must be communitarian and that nonhuman organisms, species, and ecosystems are all in some sense moral entities—that they have "interests" and "moral significance."[18] Anything which can experience "benefit" or exhibit "well-being" is understood by Johnson to have interests. Johnson's thought is teleological and, he acknowledges, inclined to be Aristotelian. But he redefines the "basic good" or "highest good" for humans as "health" in the fullest sense, and "the good life" as good, holistic functioning.[19] Surviving and thriving in concert with a multiplicity of related organisms and systems seems indeed to be, according to Johnson, optimal entelechy.

A difficulty which arises in Johnson, whose discussion of deontological and utilitarian approaches and questions of "rights," "interests," and "moral considerability" is more philosophically subtle than anything by Leopold, is the issue of preference or hierarchy. As has been indicated from Callicott's study of Leopold, it seems that Leopold (who allowed hunting, the fencing of properties, land-clearing, and some alteration of landscapes) had no great difficulty in giving preference to human interests where there might be conflicts. Leopold obviously advocated minimal disturbance to the natural environment, but humans still seem to come first. Johnson, undeniably, indicates that smallpox viruses need not have their interests served, but he resists assigning any priorities or ranking of "interests" on any basis other than "complexity." Overall, Johnson concludes that "in all instances, environmental interests must take precedence over any other interests," that it is impossible to absolutize inter-species distinctions, and that some cases require "tradeoffs" determined on a situational basis.[20]

For Johnson, perhaps even more than for Leopold, the good of the whole has priority over the good of individual parts. There are overriding biospheric interests, Johnson emphasizes,[21] and it seems that they have to be assessed intuitively. It appears that Johnson would not sacrifice a human or humans to some possible "whole," but there is nothing in him which clearly assures that. In any case, Johnson's system can be called both biocentric and ecocentric, with the clarification that he, with a number of Leopoldians and the ecofeminists, regards the Earth itself as a living organism. The Earth itself is the bio-center of his brand of biocentrism.

Alan Miller's book *Gaia Connections* runs in veins similar to those of Johnson's work, though Miller identifies himself as a "utilitarian" (whose sense of "greatest good" and "greatest number" obviously surpasses purely human measure and human concerns), and Miller is much more interested in economic ethics and the thrust toward "sustainable development" than Johnson appears to be. Miller concedes "certain natural rights" to animals, advocates an implicitly ecocentric "nonanthropocentric" ethic, but vehemently rejects biocentric egalitarianism.[22] Miller notes a debt to Leopold and J. Baird Callicott, among others, as he advocates "holistic" eco-ethical thinking. Another related thinker, self-described "rule-utilitarian" Robert Fuller, develops his ecocentric "ethics of appreciation" and of care on the premise that the Earth ecosystem makes "claims" upon humans by virtue of its status as "the one unconditioned reality on which our life is predicated."[23]

Peter Wenz finds utilitarian weighing of "benefits over burdens" inadequate as the criterion for judgment in environmental cases.[24] He critiques Rawls' *Theory of Justice* too as unhelpful in environmental decision-making because of its hypothetical "original position" and "veil of ignorance" starting point and because of the restriction of its application to people "who live together within a single society" (not the global village, it seems). Wenz finds Rawlsian justice nonextendable to nonhumans by and large, though he does believe that there may be some sort of animal "justice" possibly derivative of it.[25]

Wenz judges that wild animals ought to be seen as having "such negative rights as freedom from pain, captivity, and death *at the hands of human beings*" and that present domestic animals, animals in homes, barns, zoos, and the like (animals which he believes ought to be gradually "reintroduced to the wild"), have "positive rights to adequate food, housing, and health so long as they remain dependent on human beings."[26] In working out his theory of environmental justice, Wenz argues that moral considerability, or "direct moral concern" is owed to living individuals, species, and ecosystems. Thus he calls his stance a mix of "Biocentric Individualism" and "Ecocentric Holism." [27] Since he critiques utilitarian method, it appears that his position is, as Leopold's is claimed to be, deontological.

Wenz adopts Leopold's "communitarian" vision for his type of ecocentric holism, and he adapts Leopold's criteria of "integrity, stability, and beauty" to what Wenz calls the "integrity, stability, and diversity" of healthy ecosystems.[28] It should be evident, however, that Wenz is not strictly Leopoldian. He favors vegetarianism and opposes hunting. He draws upon Tom Regan's thinking as he develops his own perspective on "animal rights." And he appears to borrow from deep ecology's Arne Naess the principle of "nearness," which becomes in Wenz the principle of "closeness," as a guide to obligations and decisions. Wenz's model of priority is hierarchical (he calls it "concentric") in a different from usual way. He ties the strongest moral obligations to those who are "close" to humans (beings which need not necessarily be humans, then), lesser moral obligations to nondependent nonhuman animals, and even lesser ones to "nonsentient constituents of the environment." All of these constitute humans' "moral relationships," according to Wenz, and thus there are greater or lesser moral obligations to all.[29]

Roderick Nash (whose *Rights of Nature* is cited in Chapter 1) goes farther than Wenz does. Invoking the memory of Leopold,[30] Nash finds great significance in the organismic vision of the Earth and the biocentric trends of developing ecological consciousness. He proposes that there is an irreversible trend in human ethical thinking and in Western rights thinking toward the ever more inclusive. His definition of "rights" is a very nontechnical one, it should be added, bypassing moral agent-moral patient language. When he says that something or someone has "rights," Nash simply means that he, she, or it "has intrinsic worth which humans ought to respect."[31] He argues that in passing the 1973 Endangered Species Act, the United States Congress conceded rights to nature.[32] Nash is more a historian than an ethicist, but he presents the movement to perception of "inherent worth," "moral standing," and moral-legal "rights" for nonhumans as beneficial and praiseworthy.

Another self-professed Leopoldian is Van Rensselaer Potter, whose positions go considerably beyond Leopold's but are claimed by Potter as logical derivatives from Leopold's thinking. In *Global Bioethics,* Potter rejects "rights" talk to focus instead on human "responsibilities." He rather quickly moves from a consideration of the requirements of "sustainability" to the conclusion that stringent controls on human population are imperative. It should be recalled here that Leopold expressed grave concern about dense populations, but he never pursued any ideas about how to prevent prospective human population density. Potter seeks an "ecological bioethic" that promotes a "nontoxic" environment. To achieve this, he favors "controlled fertility," and he implies that governments ought to take a laissez-faire attitude toward abortion, euthanasia, selective non-treatment of illness and medical conditions, and the like. He leaves the reader with the impression that if "quality of life" choices are left to individual discernment, they promise to be more environmentally healthful.[33] Factors in such discernment must include, for Potter, population pressures and environmental impact. What seems baffling in Potter is that he seems to favor *more* governmental involvement in fertility but less in a host of other matters.

Considerably less political and polemical are the issues treated by ecocentric ethicist Holmes Rolston III. Keynotes in his writing are human-nature relations, environmental "homeostasis" (emphasizing balance, regeneration, and renewal), "value" and "values" inherent in nature, and the good of "wildness" and wilderness. From the ecosystemic vantage point, Rolston declares, "Against the standard view that value requires a *beholder,* we see how value requires only a *holder.* "[34] Like Leopold, Rolston gives the human a primacy of place (due to consciousness and conscience) but emphasizes the human's shared citizenship with all sorts of other life forms and entities. Rolston emphasizes that valuing and ethical decision-making must be widely relational, embracing nonhumans and ecosystems. Humans do, according to Rolston, have duties to sentient life, to organic life, to endangered species, and to ecosystems. They ought not inflict any suffering on animals beyond that which they would encounter in "natural" processes (which includes being efficiently killed and eaten).[35]

Since "oughts" for Rolston derive from worldview, his ethic too might be termed "visional." It is first and foremost, however, axiological in that Rolston devotes much of his writing to defining and describing the types of value in nature. His ethic is also, as Rolston terms it, "biosystemic and anthropoapical."[36] Ethical decisions are made with attentiveness to life systems and are made from the "apex" position of the human who ought to "look out for" without "looking down on" other "orders of life." The human is charged with the responsibility to do so because of humanity's cognitive, critical, and ethical faculties.[37]

"Landscapes" interact with human culture for Rolston; nature calls the human to "a spacetime, placetime ethic."[38] Harmonious, life-reverent, and "biotic community"-prizing ways of living seem, for Rolston, to constitute the "good life." A care for diversity and the Leopoldian values of "integrity, stability, and beauty" all seem to be touchstones of his ethics.

Some Closing Words on Ecocentrism

For ecocentric environmental ethics the good of humans present and future, the good of biota here and potential, and the good of ecosystems flourishing and equipped for continuity provide criteria for moral judgment. Most Leopoldians, most ecocentrists, resist absolutizing, with the possible exceptions of Wenz (who absolutizes against meat-eating and animal-keeping) and Potter (who seems to absolutize against above-zero population growth). "Intrinsic value" or "inherent value" is found in the multiplicity of beings. Value is not merely a matter of individual worth or of instrumental helpfulness to humans, though beings and things of beauty are seen as having individual worth, and usefulness to humans and service to their basic needs are certainly allowable. Value is, however, also a matter of the integral role of the variety of beings and things in ecosystems and in the Earth biosphere.

From a philosophical perception of the biodiversity that is and the organismic qualities which planet Earth seems to possess, the ecocentric "naturalists" proceed to at least one *ought:* that what is should be, to the extent possible, preserved—and preserved in such a manner that species and systems survive healthily.

The "naturalists" considered here all write from a relatively privileged American perspective. If they press for simplification of lifestyles or spend weekends in Wisconsin sand counties living in a shack, as did Aldo Leopold and his wife and children, it is a matter of preference and choice. A consideration largely missing from the ethical reflections of these thinkers is the relationship between ecological degradation and the plight of the world's poor. It is this focus which will be explored in Chapter 5.

5
Liberation Ecotheology

Dom Helder Camara, archbishop emeritus of Olinda and Recife, Brazil, has denounced as "blasphemous" humanity's usurpation of what he describes as "the power to liquidate life on our planet."[1] The school of thought which might be dubbed liberation ecotheology may not frequently denounce environmental despoliation as blasphemy, but it does share Helder Camara's analysis of the root of the problem: the perversion of human power. Ecotheology from a liberation perspective links the ruination of ecosystems with oligarchic, demagogic oppression—with what it views as the skewed assertion and enforcement of power over the poor, the landless, the voiceless, and indeed over the bounty of nature itself.

Liberation ecotheologians have in common with deep ecologists an attentiveness to the manner in which human hubris impacts nonhuman creation. With ecofeminists they share the recognition that systems of oppression wreak multivalent ill effects. With animal liberationists they acknowledge that Western habits of meat-eating and factory farming cause suffering. And they perceive with the "naturalists," or environmental holists, that the wide-ranging ecosystemic effects of human behaviors must be attended to and that wanton abuses must be halted.

An eco-ethical perspective can be said to be implicit in liberation theology across the board. Gustavo Gutiérrez, for example, has made it clear that liberation theology and liberation spirituality resist all that is "death-dealing" in the experience of poverty and affirm all that promotes the "reign of life."[2] The situation of being "dispossessed" means that persons have been cut off not only from human culture, politics, and the chance to prosper but also from right (and rightful) relations with the land itself.[3] According to Gutiérrez, the "ethics of the kingdom," elaborated in the beatitudes in the Gospel of Matthew, call the disciple to that "meekness" which receives from the land on which he or she dwells "a promise of life" and cherishes that promise.[4] The beatitudes call the disciple to that "peacemaking" which is the intentional, constructive pursuit of full "shalom." And "shalom," explains Gutiérrez, "refers to a state of wholeness and integrity, a condition of life that is in harmony with God, other people, and nature."[5]

Eco-ethical concerns, because the fate of the poor and their land are interwoven, are, then, part of the fabric of liberation theology. The heart of the matter for liberation theologians is always the "cry of the poor," and the test of human justice and Christian social ethics for liberationists must be the willingness to make the "option for the poor." This human focus does not, however, make for a narrow anthropocentrism nor necessarily what deep ecologists would call "shallow ecology." The observations of liberation theologians, even those who do not explicitly focus on environmental ethical issues, are not merely observations of how soil depletion, water pollution, and jungle clearing adversely impact humans. Instead, their remarks express repeatedly a concern for how enforced poverty and the subjugation of peoples are bound up with an assault on the natural environment.[6]

For Leonardo Boff and Sean McDonagh, ecotheology and eco-ethics have become considerably more than implicit issues or sub-themes in their explorations of the theology of liberation. Ecological issues have, instead, risen to prominence.

Boff's "New Paradigm"

From his theological reflections amid the Brazilian base communities, Leonardo Boff has moved in the 1990s into a liberation ecotheology which insists that the "option for the poor" must be extended "to include an option for the most threatened of other beings and species."[7] Boff has concluded that the social injustices wrought by the combined forces of economies designed for "unlimited growth" and governments (even supposedly democratic ones) run on a "dominant class" system[8] have further wrought "ecological injustice."[9] In presenting a proposal for "globalization," democratic socialism (a "new socialization"), and an ethics of "solidarity and communion,"[10] Boff hopes to advance an understanding of rights and mutual responsibilities among humans which embraces all of life.

Boff's *Ecology and Liberation: A New Paradigm* enunciates themes familiar in the writings of environmental holists. Boff posits the "intrinsic value" of every creature on the basis of a scientific, evolutionary worldview and on grounds of religious faith.[11] He asserts that the "new ethical order" demanded by contemporary "world-consciousness" must be "ecocentric."[12] For Boff, this means that human interests do not automatically take precedence over other interests. He insists, without elaborating a theory of rights or even defining the term, that "rights" belong to nonhuman beings—to animals, to other living species, to landforms, to air and sky, to "the environment" at large, and to the cosmos. He calls all of these beings "citizens, subject to rights" which demand respect and are due a future.[13] Boff believes that the classic notion of the "common good of humanity" must be extended so that it "includes the welfare of nature."[14]

Like the ecofeminists, Boff holds the view that hierarchical thinking and hierarchical social systems need radical restructuring. He allows that there may be a hierarchy of "function" built into nature, but he urges that hierarchies of subordination must be undone so that structures of interrelatedness and mutuality may prevail.[15] Precisely how the "new paradigm" of an ecocentric society is to be translated into customs, mores, law, systems, or operations remains unclear, but Boff envisions societies in which superpowers (of whatever ilk) are divested of their control and clout and in which choices are made to benefit those who are deprived and distressed. For Boff, crisscrossings of species and nonliving creatures constitute the disadvantaged, the marginalized, the abused, the exploited, and the endangered. A "spirituality of integration" is what Boff declares to be the needed driver of societal reconfiguration.[16] To herald what he regards as the necessary reimagining and redirecting of science, technology, global economy, politics, and religion, Boff proposes the motto "Serve life, beginning with the most threatened."[17]

The ethic which Boff presents, from his standpoint as a theologian who has long resisted the enforced suffering of the poor, might be described as one of sufficiency, synchronicity, and synergy. It is an ethic of sufficiency in the sense that access to what suffices to sustain existence is seen as the moral due of all beings. It is an ethic of synchronicity in the sense that the coincidence of contemporary cosmological theories, the Gaia hypothesis, and the retrieval of panentheistic spiritual traditions are seen as meaningful—perhaps providential—calls to attention in an era which finds itself wanting an ecological vision. It is an ethic of synergy in the sense that the interrelatedness and interactions of species, systems, and societies are seen as foundational to well-being. There are compelling reasons for Boff's ecocentrism found in the persuasiveness of the Big Bang theory and of the evolutionary story of species' development.[18] There are notably religious reasons too.

Boff interprets the divine mandate to the human as the imparting of a co-creative role in cosmic and terrestrial processes. Boff's readings of Genesis, of the Christian doctrines of the Trinity and the Holy Spirit, and his perception of the panentheistic strains in the Christian mystical tradition[19] prompt this former Franciscan to recommend a simplification of economies and lifestyles, broader representation of ecological interests in human politics, and an expanded conceptualization of rights and justice to include the environmental. As Boff sees it, liberation theology in a time of ecological crisis must be concerned simultaneously with the destitution of dwellers in South America's barrios, the abuse of indigenous peoples, the disappearance of the birds of Brazil, and "the 'hamburgerization' of the forests" in Central America and the Amazon.[20] All of these concerns are enwrapped in the Christian conviction of God's sovereignty and universal love, Boff argues.

McDonagh's "Passion"

Like Leonardo Boff, Sean McDonagh, former missioner among the T'boli in the Philippines and chair of Greenpeace, Ireland, calls for a massive overhaul of the socioeconomic order on behalf of the poorest of the poor and the convulsing planet. McDonagh's *To Care for the Earth* (1986), *The Greening of the Church* (1990), and *Passion for the Earth* (1994) all exhibit the considerable influence of the thought of Thomas Berry, with his emphasis on the transformative power of the contemporary cosmogenetic story,[21] and the eclectic creation spirituality advanced by Matthew Fox and his Institute for Culture and Creation Spirituality.[22] But his books also display McDonagh's skill at integrating the sort of environmental data found in annual *State of the World* reports and in news features with observations and experiences drawn from his years among tribal people in Mindinao.

McDonagh's method in general is to start with ecologic and economic description: exposition—and sometimes exposé—of the detrimental effects of World Bank, International Monetary Fund, and transnational corporations' policies and details of the deleterious effects of multinational trade agreements and the "structural adjustment programmes" occasioned by Third World debt. From there he proceeds to moral prescription for attitudinal and behavioral change on the part of individuals and organizations. A reordering of global priorities and a reenvisioning of human operations are, for McDonagh, critical to the survival of the most stressed of Earth's peoples and bioregions.

Like Boff, McDonagh critiques the principles and practices of capitalism. Unlike Boff, he does not counter with a proposal for an idealized socialism; instead, he calls, in a more generalized way, for more participative economic and sociopolitical structures. McDonagh's repeated recommendation is that a wholesale policy of Third World debt forgiveness or debt amnesty be inaugurated, modeled on the customs of the biblical Jubilee year recounted in Leviticus 25:23–31.[23] Like Boff, McDonagh presumes the "option for the poor" as a moral imperative, and he shows how an option for threatened lifeforms and bioregions is intimately related to the Christian preferential love for the poor. Also like Boff, McDonagh takes it as axiomatic that humans have a moral obligation to "future generations"—generations which seem, by inference, to include more than generations of *homo sapiens.*[24] McDonagh, too, uses the language of "rights," asserting as universals the "rights of other species to survive,"[25] the "rights of every other creature [along with the human] and entire ecosystems" to moral consideration,[26] and the "rights of nature" to be balanced and reconciled ethically with "human rights."[27]

The "dignity and intrinsic value" of all creatures, which McDonagh perceives as a tenet of the Genesis narrative and of Christian panentheism,[28] leads him to affirm, as Boff does, that an ecocentric rather than an anthropocentric morality is more in keeping with the biblical theology of creation and with Christian hope.[29] McDonagh finds the image of "stewardship," developed, as it has been, from the second creation story in Genesis, to be ambivalent: helpful in its emphasis on human responsibility but problematic on several counts.

For one thing, the notion of stewardship "appears to give humans some proprietary rights over the rest of creation," objects McDonagh. For another, it "implies that a creature is somehow incomplete unless it is improved upon by human hands."[30] Even more problematic, judges McDonagh, are the disjunctions between God and creation and between the human and the rest of the natural world which can be read into the idea of stewardship. The steward can be thought of as exercising management, claims McDonagh, over "a reified earth, stripped of any divine presence."[31] For these reasons, McDonagh urges that a more subtle and nuanced biblical theology of creation, one which is simultaneously theocentric and ecocentric, requires elaboration. He sees Leviticus, Job, the psalms, and the prophets as among the potential contributors to a biblical understanding of the human role as more interrelational than that of "steward."

McDonagh laments the failure of religious people, and particularly the Catholic magisterium, to attend with sufficient stridency to the problems of destitute peoples and the depleted natural world. He cites the *Catechism of the Catholic Church* as exhibiting "very little recognition of the magnitude and urgency of either the cry of the poor or the cry of the earth."[32] Like Boff, McDonagh perceives a need to promote "eco-justice" and to pursue more deliberately the realization of biblical "shalom," which he understands as "a healthy creative relationship with God and other humans, and…the well-being of all creation."[33]

The key concept for McDonagh is, as for many other environmental thinkers, "sustainability." McDonagh calls for massive individual and institutional change such that sustainability can become "the central organizing principle for every human activity."[34] The interests of the poor and the prosperous, of endangered species and prolific ones, are inextricably linked, McDonagh sees. And from his concerns for the wasted coral reefs and islands of the Philippines, he joins Boff in calling for a type of "visional" ethics which fosters the flourishing of all and demands the ceasing and desisting of those systems which degrade and deplete nature and drive peoples to desperation and death. McDonagh advocates a "pastoral ministry of sustainability" which integrates tribal peoples' rituals and celebrations of seasons and life cycles into liturgical celebrations of Christian mysteries.[35] With a more earthy liturgical and devotional life, McDonagh would also provide an intensive educational component focused on environmental responsibility and reverence.

Boff, McDonagh, and the Ecological Martyr

What Boff hopes to see arising from basic communities' reflection as praxis which achieves global dimensions, McDonagh pictures happening as large-scale institutional reform, legally enacted with some sort of consensus. Such consensus would have to be inspired by the witness of those who have opted for a more sacramental and simple life as an outcome of what they have learned from indigenous people and reclaimed from various religious resources. In somewhat different ways, both see the shift to a more ecocentric world order coming from the "bottom" up. If the writings of Boff and McDonagh are taken as types of liberation ecotheology, it is evident that both theologians have been led, inductively and from the perspective of the disadvantaged and the "powerless," to concur in the following: that an ecocentric ethic is a practical moral necessity; that it can be based in the Christian tradition; that every creature can be said to have "intrinsic value" and fundamental "rights"; and that human drives and desires for prosperity and control must be modified so that other beings might survive and thrive. Both Boff and McDonagh perceive a need for thoroughgoing reforms in economic and political systems, and they also believe that Christians must reorder priorities, refocus attention, reclaim and expand on a vibrant theology of creation, and stand prophetically with the poor, with ecosystems, and with all creatures.

To do so, however, can be, to use the familiar phrase of Dietrich Bonhoeffer, "costly grace." As liberation theologians and environmentalists know too well, the pursuit of ecojustice and the promotion of the enfranchisement of the poor can be hazardous in the extreme. Religio-political martyrdom has become almost a commonplace in areas of Central and South America. Ecological martyrdom has proved to be possible too. When liberation ecotheologians hold up a model of environmental justice and fortitude, prominent among them is Chico Mendes.

Mendes, a Brazilian rubber tapper and a kind of prototype of the indigenous popular leader, was killed in 1988 after forging a resistance movement active in the 1970s and 1980s in Amazonia. Mendes' fight was to prevent the destruction of rubber trees and to preserve the environmentally cooperative rubber tapping economy of his own people. His competitors were government agencies and business enterprises which wanted to clear the jungle. Mendes can be considered an advocate for social justice insofar as much of his movement's energy was focused on land rights and self-determination for native peoples.[36] He can also be regarded as an environmental activist insofar as the rubber tappers' resistance was also devoted to the protection of the integrity of the forest itself.[37] Mendes is remembered as a champion of "sustainability" whom Boff hails as the promoter of "an ethics of universal compassion, one that seeks harmony, respect, and concern among all creatures, not promoting the advantage of the human race."[38] Mendes resisted succumbing to a "capital gains" morality and defended his people's well established way of living simply in accord with principles of wise use and replenishment. In his own life and death, however, Mendes stands as proof that opting for the poor and for the Earth can be consumingly sacrificial. Those who engage in what Gutiérrez called "death-dealing" are capable of enacting mortal vengeance on those who are committed to the "reign of life."

Reconceiving Power

What liberation ecotheology proposes as an ideal is reverent living that affords those who might be ranked as the "underclass" their own wherewithal—the necessities for survival and opportunities for flourishing. That the "underclass" might be a human socioeconomic group or tribe *or* the nonhuman fauna, flora, waterways, and landforms of a bioregion seems to be an insight which is still quite new. Yet, as Boff and McDonagh develop the idea, it seems a logical extension and application of liberationist thought. Having arisen from the God-consciousness and the "conscientization" of the poor, liberation theology seems to be moving from implicit to explicit awareness of the linkage between the exploitation of peoples and the obliteration and exhaustion of Earth's other creatures and features. The extent of "death-dealing" is multifarious, and the range of issues which must be addressed on behalf of the "reign of life" would seem to be far-reaching and evermore complex.

A number of Northern theologians attuned to the theme of liberation have joined liberation theologians in their critiques of capitalism, consumerism, and technocracy and the obliviousness of many to the fate of the Earth. Dorothee Soelle denounces the "war against the poorest of this world, against the creation, and against ourselves"[39] which she sees being played out unthinkingly while capitalism congratulates itself on the fall of Soviet communism.

Robert McAfee Brown hails the challenge which liberation theology has posed to "First World" Christians on many counts. On the question of ecology, he notes that "pioneer work is only beginning to be done, while the clock is running out on us."[40] He calls for truthful self-confrontation, constructive anger, radical willingness to question and to rechannel energies and resources such that "churches will increasingly have to decide whether they serve God or mammon."[41]

Gibson Winter, in his *Liberating Creation,* was an early voice from the North identifying power as "the central problem of the technological age."[42] It is the issue which liberation theologians find festering wherever people are kept forcibly impoverished and subjugated and wherever riches and resources have been rendered useless—both of these, the peoples and the environment, bereft of the capacity to exercise or express their own powers.

Kyle Pasewark, in his groundbreaking *A Theology of Power,* proposes that an understanding of power "as communication of efficacy" rather than as "domination" is the more proper Christian understanding, more consonant with the notion of God as "all-powerful," more translatable into an understanding of the mutuality of being(s). That power can be understood as "being-itself" and thus grandly and gratuitously "omnipresent" wherever being is and wherever being meets being is amply defended by Pasewark.[43] That power has more often been understood as something possessed or held by some, and consequently withheld from others, seems evident from both Pasewark's study and the historical record.

The social critiques of ecofeminists and liberation theologians indicate that the human exercise of power has often been fundamentally flawed and, as a result, gravely injurious to those beings kept most "powerless." The ecological critique of social, political, and economic institutions and the patterns of thought which underlie them has further shown that power exercised as dominance, manipulation, and exploitation has undone the fiber and function of many of Earth's beings and systems. That various religious groups, including Christian churches, have also engaged in and promoted a wrongful exercise of power seems an undeniable lesson of history and of ecology. What theoretical works like Pasewark's and the praxis-oriented explorations of liberation theologians promise to do is to reexamine not only how power is and has been used and abused but also how it is and has been conceptualized. Theologies of God, creation, and anthropology are all affected by the way in which power is understood. So too, of course, are morality and ethics.

For the incipient liberation ecotheologians, for deep ecologists, ecofeminists, animal liberationists, and the "naturalists," it would seem that a reconceptualization of power and human relatedness is a pressing task for political scientists, sociologists, philosophers, and so on—but also, pressingly, for the purveyors of religious traditions. The next two chapters, then, deal with religious approaches to environmental ethical questions.

6
Eco-Ethics and the World's Religions

If there is one environmental ethical principle on which the world's religions seem to agree with near unanimity, it is that human beings ought to regard conduct conducive to the "sustainability" of the Earth as a moral imperative.

Ecological Expressions among the World's Religions

When the Parliament of the World's Religions convened in Chicago in 1993 and formulated its consensual "Declaration Toward a Global Ethic," it included in its commitment to "a culture of non-violence, respect, justice, and peace" strong environmental notes.

It affirmed those "ancient guidelines for human behaviours which are found in the teachings of the religions of the world and which are the conditions for a sustainable world order." It spoke of the "interdependent" nature of the "whole" of life and emphasized "respect for the community of living beings" and "preservation of Earth, the air, water and soil."[1]

The signatories of the elaborated declaration included Bahais, Brahma Kumaris, and a wide range of Orthodox, Protestant, and Catholic Christians; Hindus, Jains, Jews and Moslems; practitioners of African and Native American tribal religions; Sikhs, Taoists, Theosophists, and Zoroastrians; neo-pagans and the representatives of a variety of interreligious organizations. Thus, the subscribers counted among them Brother David Steindl-Rast, O.S.B., and His

Royal Highness Oseijeman Adefunmi I; Rev. Deborah Ann Light and Professor Susannah Heschel; Honorable Louis Farrakhan and Cardinal Joseph Bernardin; the Dalai Lama and Rev. Dr. Syngman Rhee; Dr. Thelma Adair and Maria Svolos Gebhard; Professor Hans Küng and Rev. Baroness Cara-Marguerite-Drusilla.[2] Nearly two hundred representatives of an array of religious traditions came together to assent to "four universal directives," which are also termed "four broad, ancient guidelines," for a "new global order."[3]

Of particular interest to those who hold that there is a "natural law" inscribed in the human heart is the fact that the "four irrevocable directives" arise from what this Parliament takes to be axiomatic: that "every human is obliged to behave in a genuinely human fashion, to **do good and avoid evil.**"[4] Students of Thomas Aquinas will recall that, in Thomas, the "first precept of law" states "that good is to be done and pursued, and evil is to be avoided" (ST I–II.94.2). This is regarded by Thomas, in this article of the *Summa Theologica,* as the basis for all other precepts of the natural law.

The "four irrevocable directives" of the *Global Ethic* elaborate on: 1) a "commitment to a culture of non-violence and respect for life"; 2) a "commitment to a culture of solidarity and a just economic order"; 3) a "commitment to a culture of tolerance and a life of truthfulness"; and 4) a "commitment to a culture of equal rights and partnership between men and women."[5] Expressing abhorrence of the escalation of crime, ethnic and tribal warfare, abuse, and oppression, this declaration by adherents to a host of world religions calls upon their memberships, and indeed all the world's peoples, to make strenuous efforts at peacemaking, cross-cultural cooperation, social justice, empowering the disadvantaged, and preserving the Earth's ecosystems and resources.

The declaration seems to suggest that those actions which despoil the Earth and those which dehumanize its populace are of a piece. Violence, inhumanity, and deception in manifold forms are seen as wreaking havoc on a global scale, and the "new global order" which is called for is seen as demanding concrete actions against brutality and deceit. The document, which makes stern condemnations and strident affirmations, invites people everywhere to commit themselves "to understanding one another, and to socially-beneficial, peace-fostering, and nature-friendly ways of life."[6]

As Hans Küng has amply explained, the document is spiritual

in tone but decidedly not theocentric.[7] The reader of the Parliament's declaration could defensibly describe it as human-centered insofar as it calls
for profound human responsibility and "spiritual renewal" and "conversion of heart."[8] But the worldview, despite the focus of many of the declaration's elaborations on human concerns, seems more rightly termed
biocentric. This telling passage reveals the biocentrism of the 1993
Global Ethic:

> A human person is infinitely precious and must be uncondi-
> tionally protected. But likewise the **lives of animals and
> plants** which inhabit this planet with us deserve protection,
> preservation, and care. Limitless exploitation of the natural
> foundations of life, ruthless destruction of the biosphere,
> and militarization of the cosmos are all outrages.[9]

This statement of the fundamental entitlement of living things to "protection, preservation, and care" seems to arise from an underlying conviction of the intrinsic value of living things—and notably of nonhuman
living things. According to the declaration, humans assuredly have
moral obligations to their own species, but they are understood to inhabit
a larger world of life which ought not to be violated.

In the statement which immediately follows this passage in the
declaration, there is also an indication that present humans have obligations to those yet to be born. While the document does not specifically
say that future generations have "rights," it clearly urges that present
humans have *duties* to them: "As human beings we have a special
responsibility—especially with a view to future generations—for Earth
and cosmos, for the air, water, and soil."[10]

It would also seem arguable that the vision of the Parliament of
the World's Religions moves from the primarily biocentric to the ecocentric, by extension. There is a sense that the whole of the Earth *oikos,*
and indeed the whole of the *kosmos,* is the proper concern of humans—
and not merely because they support life. The declaration continues:

> We are **all intertwined together** in this cosmos and we are all
> dependent on each other. Each one of us depends on the wel-
> fare of all. Therefore the dominance of humanity over nature

and the cosmos must not be encouraged. Instead we must cultivate living in harmony with nature and the cosmos.[11]

The Parliament carefully avoids speaking of human "dominion" over the Earth even while it eschews the idea of "dominance." It turns instead to the ideal of "harmony" with living things, natural phenomena, and the cosmos itself. There are no ethical prescriptions about what to do in hard cases, about how to resolve moral dilemmas. But there is the upholding of an ethical ideal which chooses the best for the whole and considers not only present but future beings. Individualism, "speciesism," and short-range cost-benefit thinking are proscribed.

The declaration certainly does not develop a consensual theological or spiritual anthropology. It does, however, assert that every human being ought to have "an equal chance to reach full potential as a human being."[12] A pervasive conviction of the document seems to be that all of life, the planet itself, and the cosmos too ought to flourish. Without ascribing any specific divine directedness to life or the cosmos, the document expresses the idea that self-fulfillment, continuity, and maximal development are the proper teleology of all beings.

It can be noted that there is, then, an ethic of being, becoming, and letting-be which characterizes the consensus of the Parliament of the World's Religions. The *Global Ethic* does not insist that endangered species must all be preserved, nor does it suggest that wetlands, forests, or jungles ought to stand unaltered. What it *does* do is to propose not a prescriptive ethic but a descriptive one. The declaration indicates that where a multiplicity of lifeforms coexist and flourish harmoniously, where landscapes are not being devastated and resources are not being toxified, good is being done. Behaviors that nurture life and advance interdependence are seen as praiseworthy. Where ecosystems function to the benefit of their individual parts as well as to the well-being of the whole, "the better" is seen as prevailing.[13]

The biocentric and ecocentric vision expressed in *A Global Ethic* is hardly surprising in light of the work done in recent years by ethical thinkers from many religious traditions who have confronted environmental questions. From the late 1960s on, there have been recurrent statements concerning a general "Oriental" approach to ecological issues. Taoism, Buddhism, Confucianism, Jainism, and Hinduism have been explored for their environmental implications. While it is impossible to group these genuinely, it should be noted that the religions of the East in general tend to de-center the role of the human. Tu Wei-Ming suggests that these religions advocate a "less adversarial, less individualistic, and less self-interested" approach to civilization than Western traditions seem to have.[14] Harmonious living and humility are keynotes of these religions. And the theme of "sustainability" appears and reappears.[15]

Gandhian "nonviolence *(ahimsa)* and nonpossession *(aparigraha)*" are seen as bound up with Hindu and Jain attitudes of "inherent respect for the nonhuman realms of existence."[16] Mahayana Buddhism holds that "all animate beings" at least have "the inherent potentiality…to attain the supreme and perfect enlightenment of Buddhahood" and thus ought to be regarded reverently.[17] A perception of "the universality of organic process" also seems intrinsic to Buddhism, as is the sense of "the cosmic body of the Buddha."[18] Egocentrism and an anthropocentrism which disregards the fullness of Being of the multiform potential for Buddhahood is delusion and illusion.

Taoism has often been hailed as ideal for its ecological sympathies.[19] Mary Evelyn Tucker has asserted that: "While Taoism and Confucianism are quite different in their specific teachings, they share a worldview that might be described as organic, vitalistic, and holistic."[20] Nature is regarded as possessing worth, or value, "for its own sake," and human interference should be minimal, if not nil, in Taoist thinking.[21] Confucianism emphasizes the interrelationship of the "human order" and the "natural order" and strives for a balanced, reciprocal ideal.[22]

Islam too has been claimed to be environmentally responsible because of the way in which it decenters the role of the human. While Islam presents the human as one enjoying a certain primacy of place over other creatures by Allah's design, there is a radical theocentrism to Islam's vision of creation. Since all is created by Allah and all is dependent on Allah, the human rule over other creatures can hardly be seen as "dominion." It is, suggests Roger Timm, more a call to "gratitude."[23] Timm goes on to explain:

> Allah bestows authority over creation on humans, not as an absolute right to do as they please, but as a test—a test of their obedience, loyalty, and gratitude to God. Abusing the earth violates the will of Allah; caring for it fulfills God's will. From this perspective, human vicegerency means

exercising responsible care for the environment, not violating or exploiting it.[24]

Native religions, tribal religions, de-center the human in their own way. In their animism and/or polytheism, the human is subject to a variety of spiritual forces, forces which inhabit and permeate the grasses and trees, the grazing and fleet-foot creatures, beings which fly and swim, waters which surge, and winds that whistle. Living peaceably, and even at times appeasingly, among these inspirited beings is part of the wisdom of life. Human arrogance or ignorance of the withinness of things can prove deadly. Earth processes and cosmic events proceed in the realm of mystery, and present generations are merely a part of a long chain of ancestors which runs on to unknown descendants. Trespassing beyond boundaries seems, among tribal religions, to be sin, crime, tragedy, and often the Earth itself rebels against human trespass.[25]

There is good reason, then, for a number of the world's religions to arrive at a nonanthropocentric ecological vision and to assert the intrinsic value of nonhuman creation and the moral considerability of present beings, present natural forms, and also future generations. The sticking point on religion-ecology discussions has seemed to be, from the late 1960s on, the assertions about the human made in the Judaeo-Christian tradition and that tradition's associations with what has increasingly been seen as the mechanistic, manipulative tendencies of Western life and thought.

The Lynn White Thesis and the Response

In 1967 historian Lynn White published a now renowned—and much disputed—article, "The Historical Roots of Our Ecologic Crisis." As White scanned the mounting record of environmental damages, he, like many others, sought to understand the causes. The thesis he proposed was that the Judaeo-Christian tradition, with its emphasis on God's transcendence, the other-worldly destiny of the human, its orientation toward "progress," and its biblical notion of human "dominion" over the Earth, bore much of the blame for environmental devastation and degradation. The tradition fostered a perception of nature as "other," White argued, and allowed for a very exploitive exercise of "dominion."[26]

Ever since Professor White's leveling of this charge, Jews and Christians, biblical scholars, ethicists, and systematic theologians have taken pains to examine and elaborate a scriptural theology of creation and to scrutinize the writings of religious leaders and scholars whose statements might have environmental implications. Eric Katz concludes that the Jewish tradition does not endorse "unbridled domination." Instead, the Torah and long tradition teach that "humanity is the steward of the natural world, not its owner." God is "owner" and sovereign.[27] As Katz explains it, Judaic stewardship presumes that humans act as "partners in the never-ending task of perfecting the universe."[28] It does not require heroic efforts of the human, but it does expect ordinary justice and prudence. Katz summarizes thus: "The concept of stewardship in Judaism advocates neither the *domination-destruction* nor the *preservation* of the natural environment but its conservation and wise developmental use."[29] As Katz interprets it, the Jewish tradition must be understood as promoting a theocentric view of nature which embraces a kind of mild anthropocentrism, wherein humanity is not be-all and end-all but has the right to use creation and to make judgments about how its beauty and serviceability might be conserved. Nature and creatures do not seem so much possessed of intrinsic value as endowed with value. Their value is derivative of the Creator-God who is their owner. Katz thus suggests that nonhuman beings have a "sacred" quality in Judaism because they are the sacred "property" of God.[30]

What Katz points up is that Judaism can be understood as very environmentally friendly. Ancient prescriptions concerning land treatment and harvesting, sewage disposal, and the slaughter of animals, along with the millennia-long singing of psalms which celebrate the splendor of creation, tend to impress upon believers the importance of sound ecological behavior. But there is no decided ecocentric thrust, and the extent of obligations to nature and creatures remains somewhat unclear. It is easy to see why the Judaic creation tradition can be apprehended as ambivalent.

The Christian tradition has clearly been identified as both ambiguous and ambivalent with regard to the natural world, though there have been fervent efforts on the part of Christian groups to renounce these tendencies in the tradition. Paul Santmire, a Lutheran pastor, has shown in *The Travail of Nature: The Ambiguous Ecological Promise of Christian Theology* that the Christian tradition is fraught with a mix of negative and positive motifs: disdain for the body, the Earth, and matter and a desire for pure transcendence and spiritualization; incarnational, resurrectional, eschatological thought that incorporates flesh and spirit, creation and cosmic destiny; earthen images and metaphors which inspire and dismay. Santmire concludes that the best remedy for the tradition's ambiguity is the deliberate adoption, on the part of Christians, of "an ecological reading of biblical faith."[31] This presumes a renunciation of dualistic, Earth-denying, disembodying biblical interpretation and tendencies in the tradition.

The task of reclaiming and reframing Christian attitudes toward creation has led biblical scholars to explore the oft-neglected or understated creation theology of the Bible. A plethora of works exploring traditional Christian themes and hoping to have formative impact on incipient ecological-mindedness among Christians have also emerged. These include theological reflection on creation and proposals for ethical action. They examine beliefs and behaviors as they affect Christians of a variety of denominations. A sampling of these includes: *Covenant for a New Creation: Ethics, Religion, and Public Policy* (1991), authored by Carol S. Robb, a seminary professor of Christian social ethics, and Carl J. Casebolt, a minister of the United Church of Christ and a health-and-environment advocate for the National Council of Churches; *Keeping and Healing the Creation* (1989) and *Restoring Creation for Ecology and Justice* (1990), a handbook and a church-wide report and resolution for conscience-formation and environmental action issued at the prompting of the Eco-Justice Task Force of the Presbyterian Church (U.S.A.); *Ecological Healing: A Christian Vision* (1993), assembled by Nancy G. Wright and Donald Kill for CODEL, a Protestant, Catholic, and Orthodox group called Coordination for Development, Inc., which focuses on the concerns of the poor and promotes "sustainable" development and environmental protection in impoverished countries. All of these attest to an effort on the part of Christians to restore, and in some cases revise, biblical covenant motifs and understandings of human vocation such that relations with God, other humans, and all of creation are seen as integrally linked. A vision which might be called *concentric,* coordinating theocentrism, anthropocentrism, and ecocentrism, seems to be clarifying for a number of Christian groups. Such a vision would seem to be a way out of ambiguity.

At the forefront of organized Christian action and reflection on environmental issues has been the World Council of Churches. In the

1970s the council's Church and Society division produced a document on "Just, Participatory and Sustainable Society." In the 1980s and 1990s the council has regularly issued materials and created programs for "Justice, Peace, and Integrity of Creation."[32] The WCC has made a commitment to sustainability as a worthy environmental goal, and many member churches have undertaken efforts on behalf of the environment as part of their "mission." Concerns about the links "between ecology and economy" and "the interdependence between the protection of creation and the demand for justice" have found expression in repeated WCC gatherings and statements.[33]

In framing the World Council's programs and proclamations, the biblical witness has been studied and its creation theology reexamined. The theme of the activity of the Holy Spirit in creation has been explored. Inevitably, considerable differences of opinion have emerged as member churches have inquired into how, precisely, the role of the human vis-à-vis nature ought to be understood, how pervasive the impact of the "fall" is regarded, and how faith in God's transcendence as well as God's immanence ought to be expressed. All of these issues impinge on a developing theology of creation which emphasizes its "integrity" and the human responsibility toward worldly wholeness and creaturely health.

The theme of the World Council's 1991 General Assembly was "Come Holy Spirit, Renew the Whole Creation," and a report to the Justice, Peace, and Integrity of Creation division was contributed to by John Cobb, Jr., Jay McDaniel, Sallie McFague, Tom Regan, and many others whose work has been at the forefront of environmental ethics and creation theology. The Council considered "a theology for the liberation of life" which included such themes as the unity of the world, the intrinsic value of creatures, the good of diversity, the responsibility of the human for establishing good "order" in creation, a wide-ranging reverence for life, a call for lifestyles which advance sustainability, and a concern for the conditions which cry out for a kind of environmental justice. The latter included a plea for attention to the plight of the world's impoverished peoples and also to the conditions of the world's animals.[34] Like the work of the Parliament of the World's Religions, this report can be said to be biocentric, in that it is very attentive to the situation of all living things (and especially so to animals), but also ecocentric, in that it looks to larger questions of ecosystems and planetary survival. In the sense that it locates the responsibility for action in the reflective, faith-filled human, it can be said to be anthropocentric—but, again, only mildly or "weakly" so. The report is, overall, theocentric as it expresses its themes in terms of strong biblical faith in a creating, provident God, in Jesus as "cosmic Christ," and in the Spirit "who works in and through the whole creation."[35]

A strong direction in the World Council, then, has been toward a trinitarian theology of creation. René Coste has provided an account of the commitments to which the World Council had already "covenanted" its members by 1990, the year before the Cobb-McDaniel-McFague-Regan-etc. report was produced. Out of its theologies of creation and of the moral order, the WCC pledged itself to four commitments which are summarized here: 1) an economic order which would benefit all and would relieve peoples from "the slavery of all external debt" (an issue which Sean McDonagh links to ecological devastation, as Chapter 5 of this book points out); 2) an international order dedicated to peace-keeping and promoting "a culture of nonviolence as a force for change and liberation"; 3) a respect for the Earth which will be particularly alert to the atmosphere and problems of climate change; 4) an end to various forms of discrimination, particularly racism.[36]

The World Council's efforts have not gone unhindered. Perhaps the two greatest stumbling blocks to agreement among the member churches attempting to frame an appropriate Earth-ethic have been a mistrust of human efforts in general (held very strongly in some expressions of the Reformed tradition) and the aforementioned differences about the extent of the effects of original sin on the created order. Despite these, the World Council has advanced strong theoretical and practical statements on environmental issues and has succeeded in linking, for most of its members, inquiry into environmental ethics with Christian discipleship. A very optimistic interpretation of the efforts of the WCC through 1994 is offered in this expression of their work by Larry Rasmussen: "'Ecumenical' does indeed mean the whole inhabited world—humankind and otherkind together in a precarious and undeniable unity of life and death. And 'ecumenics' means realizing right relationship among the diverse members of the household so as to foster the flourishing of life for all."[37]

Some Conclusions about Religious Eco-Ethics

What appears to be emerging, among the many and diverse inter-religious and ecumenical discussions of the environment, is an ethic that emphasizes a positive vision of the natural world and a conscientious commitment to pro-environment action on the part of individual believers and religious organizations. Humans, animals, fields, forests, jungles, rivers, lakes, seas, and ecosystems are all deemed—in varying ways and to varying degrees—worthy of moral consideration and respect. The motivations for such moral consideration and for conserving and/or preserving commitments are both humane and religious.

David Hallman, an officer for energy and environment with the United Church of Canada and a participant in WCC and United Nations environmental dialogues and events (such as the Rio "Earth Summit"), has observed the "one Earth" motifs that span discussions and position statements. Whether the declaration of the Parliament of the World's Religions, the work of ecotheologians or religious eco-ethicists, the recommendations of the Presbyterian Eco-Justice Task Force, CODEL, or the WCC are under consideration, it seems obvious that, as Hallman notes, each body's "theology propels us into ethics." Many religious bodies are concluding this with him: "Living in a spiritual relation with creation requires a different life-style."[38]

If not unanimously ecocentric, many of the world's religions seem to be concluding that the good life must be nonviolent, nonexploitive, nonabusive, biota-reverent, life-restorative, and ecosystemic.

7
Eco-Ethics and the
Catholic Magisterium

At the close of the June 1995 meeting of the U.S. Catholic bishops, Archbishop Daniel E. Pilarczyk is reported to have suggested that the bishops save papers and materials yet to be acted on and return for their November 1995 gathering with those materials in hand. Cardinal William Keeler of Baltimore, the conference president, was quoted as replying, "The chair, with extreme ecological sensitivity, agrees," and the bishops were duly sent forth with paper-saving instructions.[1] Shortly after the bishops' June meeting, their national office for Environmental Justice announced the availability of a resource packet called "Peace with God the Creator, Peace with All Creation" for parish use.[2]

That same summer the bishops hosted a consultation on "Ecology and Catholic Theology: Contribution and Challenge," an event which resulted in the late 1996 issuance of *"And God Saw That It Was Good": Catholic Theology and the Environment*. This essay collection includes scholarly and prayerful considerations of the theology of creation, Christian eschatology, the science-theology dialogue on cosmological questions, sacramental theology, the monastic tradition, and moral theology's core concepts of human dignity, the common good, and virtue and shows the relevance of all of these to present ecotheological and eco-ethical reflection. It also appends environmental statements by Pope John Paul II and a number of bishops' conferences (the United States, Australia, the Dominican Republic, Guatemala, northern Italy, the Philippines), along with other helpful materials.[3]

78

Both the lighter episode and the more serious issuance of resources highlight a growing trend toward environmental pronouncements and environmental prescriptions on the part of the Roman Catholic magisterium.

Ecological Hints in Vatican II

The Vatican II pastoral constitution *Gaudium et Spes* laid a foundation for environmental reflection by noting the paradox found in the church's understanding of the human.[4] The human is, by his or her "innermost nature," a "social being," made in God's image, given dominion over "all earthly creatures" with a right to "subdue them and use them to God's glory" (GS #12). Yet the human is also one who, because of sin, has fallen "out of harmony with himself, with others, and with all created things" (GS #13). Called to attend to and advance the "universal common good" (GS #84), humans bear reminding that caring for and "cultivating" the Earth is a human obligation (GS #39). Humane and fructifying "development" of the Earth is part of "the design of God" (GS #57). Modern warfare, highly technologized and "aimed indiscriminately at the destruction of entire cities or of extensive areas along with their population," is seen as "crime" and "abomination" (GS #80). Actions which smack of deliberate Earth-devastation are seen as ungodly and anti-human.

In the years since the close of the Council, more specific and pointed references to Earth care have come from bishops' conferences, popes, and Vatican offices. They have in common the ecologically conscious yet decidedly anthropocentric tone of *Gaudium et Spes*. While most fundamentally theocentric, because of its theology of creation, the Catholic magisterial view is also thoroughgoing in its anthropocentrism insofar as it focuses on the human as *imago Dei,* as the being charged with responsible "dominion" over the Earth, as the moral agent capable of prudently using or flagrantly misusing other created beings and resources. The human occupies a primacy of place in the created order in Catholic thought. Yet other creatures have their own place and "proper perfection" (an expression grounded in Thomas Aquinas).[5] As environmental concerns have increasingly occupied the magisterium, a theory of creaturely value and an ethic of creaturely respect (though not a concession of animals' or nature's "rights") have marked magisterial writings. The end or telos of the human is clearly seen as a final union with God in eternity, but creation itself and the diversity of creatures are seen as having their own proper ends: surviving and thriving in accord with the divine design.

The Statements of John Paul II

The encyclicals of John Paul II, the utterances of bishops' conferences, and points made in the *Catechism of the Catholic Church* would seem to bear out these themes: 1) a vision of the natural world that is theocentric and anthropocentric but also, in some senses, incipiently ecocentric out of a reverence for all of creation's expression of the divine being; 2) a sense that other-than-human beings possess "intrinsic value" even while they fittingly have "instrumental value" to humans; 3) an understanding that humans are obligated to use and care for animals and the whole Earth respectfully; 4) a morality which implicates human agency in consequences not only to present but to future generations; 5) a view of the human telos as not only God-driven but intertwined with other living beings, the planet, and the cosmos; 6) a life-ethic that prescribes care, prudent use, the exercise of foresight and restraint in environmentally impacting actions and that locates responsibility for environmentally ethical attitude formation and behavior in all manner of societal institutions: churches, civic communities, businesses, schools, professional organizations, farm policy makers, international economic systems, land and resource managers.

Beginning with his inaugural encyclical, *Redemptor Hominis,* Pope John Paul II has enunciated a theocentric anthropocentrism. He has repeated in subsequent encyclicals this initial maxim: "[M]an is the primary route that the Church must travel in fulfilling her mission: *he is the primary and fundamental* way for the Church."[6] To deep ecologists, ecofeminists, and the otherwise anti-anthropocentric, this would suggest that the pope is hopelessly insensitive and irretrievably "shallow" ecologically. It should be noted, however, that the pope prefaces the maxim with a strong expression of concern over the militarizing, industrializing, and technologizing tendencies of "the world 'groaning in travail'" (RH #8).

His social encyclicals in particular pick up environmental ethical themes. In *Sollicitudo Rei Socialis,* John Paul II widens the scope of discussion of "respect for life" by insisting that such "respect" includes the world of nature. An awareness of the limits of resources and a "need to respect the integrity and the cycles of nature" must be factored into projects for "development," the pope urges, cautioning against "superdevelopment" and profligate consumerism.[7]

A holistic vision of creation is advanced in this encyclical, a vision of the "cosmos" as an orderly unity which impinges upon humans the obligation to be aware of the interdependence of "the different categories of being, whether living or inanimate—animals, plants, the natural elements" and to recognize that humans cannot disrupt or break that order and interconnection wantonly (SRS #34). The pope admonishes readers not to exhaust nonrenewable resources and holds that refraining from activities which pollute the environment are among the "moral demands" upon humanity (SRS #34). John Paul II, in this encyclical, upholds the biblical vision of human "dominion" but makes it clear that it is a limited dominion. The realm of human "relationship" for him is a wide one: "with self, neighbor, with even the remotest human communities, and with nature itself...." (SRS #38).

In the 1991 encyclical *Centesimus Annus,* John Paul II further refines his understanding of human "dominion." While asserting that humans can and should collectively "dominate the earth,"[8] and that they ought to do so equitably, he describes "dominion" as the task of the human as "cooperator with God in the work of creation." When people go about this task haphazardly and destructively, they are guilty of "provoking a rebellion on the part of nature," and they leave the natural world "more tyrannized than governed" (CA #37). The same passage makes a clear assertion of the "intrinsic value" of nonhuman creation. The pope observes, in cautionary tones: "People think that they can make arbitrary use of the earth, subjecting it without restraint to their wills, as though the earth did not have its own requisites and a prior God-given purpose, which human beings can indeed develop but must not betray" (CA #37). This is hardly "biocentric egalitarianism," but it is a forthright endorsement of the "intrinsic value" or "inherent worth" of nonhuman beings.

In extolling the "truth" and the "beauty" to be found in creation, the pontiff also responds to another environmental ethical issue. He unequivocally affirms that "humanity today must be conscious of its duties and obligations towards future generations" (CA #54). As moral agents who can foresee consequences over the long range, humans are seen by the pope as charged with a preservationist and protectionist obligation on behalf of those who will come after them. He does not assert, but also seems not to exclude the possibility, that "future genera-tions" might be seen as including beings other than humans. John Paul II thus clearly promotes, in this encyclical, the idea of duties to future gen-erations, and he suggests that actions on behalf of endangered species ought to be taken so that their "God-given purpose" is not "betrayed."

The encyclical on the moral life, *Veritatis Splendor,* is not partic-ularly occupied with ecological issues, but it does speak of the moral agent as a person in relationship with creation, linked through the Old Covenant to the land, and impelled toward "peaceful harmony with the Creator and with all creation."[9]

In *Evangelium Vitae,* his 1995 encyclical on "The Gospel of Life," John Paul II makes more significant environmental points. Using the murder of Abel by Cain as the archetypal crime against life, the pope makes this observation: "Murderous violence profoundly changes the environment."[10] The land itself becomes desolate and fruitless as a result of human violence. As he enumerates the multiplicity of forms of "murder, war, slaughter and genocide" afflicting humanity, the pope establishes linkages between "an unjust distribution of resources," along with "reckless tampering with the world's ecological balance," and a more generalized "violence against life" (EV #10).

The pope upholds a hierarchical anthropology which hails the human as "'mysteriously different' from other earthly creatures" and ascribes to an atheistic egalitarianism any self-diminishment of *homo sapiens* which might lead to license and to the treatment of life as "a mere 'thing.'" The pope goes on to assert that disconnection from God and from a conviction of human godliness is of a piece with a discon-nection from the world of creation. "Nature itself, from being 'mater' (mother)," he says, "is now reduced to being *'matter,'* and is subjected to every kind of manipulation" (EV #22).

There are, however, hopeful life-signs, the pope suggests. Present-ing a "seamless garment" ethic, he lauds pro-life activism, life-preserva-tive medical advances, institutions of care, commitments to nonviolence, opposition to capital punishment, and "the growing attention being paid to the *quality of life* and to *ecology"* as salutary (EV #27). He reiterates his previously stated convictions concerning human responsibility to future generations and speaks for a temperate exercise of "dominion" (EV #42). It can be observed, over all, that Pope John Paul II advocates an ethic of environmental responsibility, reverence, and restraint.[11]

Bishops Speaking for the Environment

Amid the production of these papal encyclicals, a number of bishops' conferences have issued statements and pastoral letters pertaining to the environment. One, the Filipino letter cited in the Introduction to this book, is noteworthy for its stunning presentation of the preservation of the environment as "the ultimate pro-life issue." Citing scripture side by side with comment on Philippine forests and coral reefs, the bishops call for a reversal of abuses, a renunciation of ruinous military and industrial practices, and a restoration of the land. They listen to the testimony of church tradition and the testimony of island peoples. They set forth as examples Mary, the "Mother of Life," and the Chipko women, who are noted in Chapter 2 of this text, as models for ecological action. Like the pope, they proffer a vision of interdependence and communion in a "relationship which links God, human beings and all the community of the living."[12]

In 1991 the Catholic Bishops of the United States issued a comprehensive ecological statement, "Renewing the Earth." It is a strong visional statement, presenting the notion of "a sacramental universe—a world which discloses the Creator's presence by visible and tangible signs." This "sacramental universe" elicits, or ought to, an attendant reverence and "human accountability for the fate of the earth."[13] The bishops adapt the phrase of Pope John XXIII and Vatican II, the "universal common good," to discuss "the planetary common good." They call for "a new solidarity" transnationally, an "option for the poor" which acknowledges the relationship between ecological and economic well-being, an "authentic development" which fosters "moderation and even austerity" in productivity and possessions. They caution against overconsumption and enjoin "responsible parenthood," via natural family planning, as they address population issues.[14]

The U.S. bishops regard "respect for life" as broadly inclusive, and they allude to Thomas Aquinas' teachings concerning the good of creaturely diversity and multiplicity (ST I.47.1, unreferenced). The perception of a "web of life" marks the bishops' observations on the frequent chain-reaction effects of political, military, technological, and corporate decisions as well as the environmental impact of individuals' personal habits and lifestyles.

A set of "oughts" and "ought nots" can be garnered from papal and episcopal statements. They include the more generalized "ought" of holding a reverent, sacramental vision of creation and an appropriately responsible and humble vision of the human. The "oughts" of simplifying lifestyles, cutting back consumption, participating in efforts to protect ecosystems and preserve endangered species, and advancing more just distribution of the world's goods and resources are implicitly and explicitly stated. General "ought nots" concerning abuse and misuse are enunciated. Education, advocacy, and worship all seem to be linked as preventives of environmental exploitation in the magisterial mind. Attention to the biblical theology of creation and to the practice of saints like Francis of Assisi (often mentioned) or Philip Neri (mentioned in the *Catechism*) is encouraged and urged.

The Environment and the Catechism

The 1990s' *Catechism of the Catholic Church* presents a christocentric and trinitarian vision of creation which conceives of human "dominion" as a ministry on behalf of creaturely "harmony" and as a role of "stewardship."[15] The Thomistic notion that "creation has its own goodness and proper perfection" (#302) implies a belief in the "intrinsic value" of all creatures and of creation in general. The catechism does, in fact, point to the "particular goodness of every creature" (#339) and the necessity for human respect for that particular good. Diversity, beauty, the "interdependence of creatures," and creaturely solidarity are hailed as signs of the Creator and of the divine will (#340–#344). The integrity of creation, the common good, limited human dominion, and the benefit of future generations are all cited as human concerns (#2415).

How human responsibility is rightly played out is treated in the catechism under the matter of the seventh commandment and its injunction against stealing. A surprising amount of attention is paid to animals in this section of the catechism. A hierarchical order of the human as *imago Dei* and the animal as a creature intended for the service of the human (a vision in which the Catholic tradition is steeped) is preserved here, but with notable qualifications. The catechism asserts the rightfulness of human use of animals for food, clothing, assistance in work or leisure, and in medical and scientific experiments which are conducted "within reasonable limits" (#2417). Inflicting pain on animals or causing their deaths needlessly is seen as an affront to "human dignity," as something which predisposes people to cruelty to humans as well (#2418)—an idea also indebted (though not acknowledged) to the thought of Thomas Aquinas (SCG III.112.13 and ST I–II.102.6 ad 8). An interesting turn is taken when the catechism cautions against an excess quite the opposite of cruelty to animals too: excessive love for or spending on pets (#2418).

Animals, in the catechism, are not said to have "rights," but it is clear that there are right and wrong actions of which they may be recipients. That is to say, the catechism seems to regard them as "moral patients."[16] Animals, along with other resources, are seen as due consideration in the fulfillment of humans' "moral obligations...including those toward generations to come" (#2456). Like John Paul II, then, the catechism deems nonhuman creation worthy of what philosophers have called "moral considerability" and leaves open, by the very nonspecificity of "generations to come," the possibility that there may be moral obligations not only to future humans but to other creatures with a potential future.

For religious reasons contemporary Catholic magisterial voices lend support to an ethic of sustainability.[17] They prescribe respectful and "reasonable" use of nonhuman creation, special care to prevent needless pain, injury, or death to animals, a preservationist approach to biodiversity, simple and even abstemious lifestyles, and a host of careful behaviors implicit in the notion of "stewardship." Catholicism clearly takes a hierarchical view of creation; nevertheless, it sees the primacy of the human as a call to "cooperate" in and with creation rather than as a license to exploit and exhaust.

Environmental Issues and Eco-Friendly Traditions

Catholicism today is engaged in a recovery of a variety of pro-environment traditions: the Franciscan,[18] the Benedictine,[19] and the

Thomistic[20] among them. As it reflects on these, with the biblical creation tradition and the traditions of Catholic social thought, the church seems to be arriving at conclusions most closely allied with those of what this book calls the "naturalist" school. It does so, however, out of a trinitarian and incarnational theology, a theology of divine interrelatedness and divine immersion in the world of water, wind, and flesh.

The great sticking point for a nascent Catholic environmental ethic is, of course, the question of population. Most environmental ethical thinkers and most environmentalists, it seems safe to say, favor extensive efforts at birth limitation and the slowing of population growth. The church's difficulties with the rather general acceptance of artificial contraception, and sometimes of abortion, as pragmatic routes to the achievement of zero population growth are well known. Van Rensselaer Potter has blasted the pope for "advocating a course irrevocably committed to irresponsible and, indeed, miserable survival in terms of net results" because of his refusal to endorse artificial contraception.[21]

Potter may not, however, have the last word in the dialogue—or lack thereof—on the question of population limitation. Magisterial discussion of "responsible parenthood" has, at least, resulted in what seemed at one time an unthinkable promotion of natural family planning and has encouraged the spacing of births and delaying of pregnancies for a variety of conscientious reasons—including the limited availability of resources. One or two Catholic thinkers who might be described as pursuants of ecospirituality and as political "liberals" have voiced a preference for natural family planning as ecologically sound routes to forestalling population pressures.[22] The idea of harmony with natural processes rather than chemical or instrumental interventions has an occasional appeal to those who favor solar energy, herb gardens, and less technology-intensive living patterns, it appears.

Some ecofeminists too have expressed mistrust of technology, the inventions of "technocrats," and "artificiality" when these are foisted on women.[23] There is also some ecofeminist wariness of the possible denigration of the woman's capacities as "bearer of life" in the zero population growth movement.[24] That is not to say that there is any great applause for the Catholic magisterial position, but it is to say that considerably more discussion on the role of the "natural" in population questions and as a means to "sustainability" may be anticipated. The Catholic magisterium may continue to be viewed as an arch-foe of what is practical and expedient in its allowance only of natural family planning as birth-preventer. And other environmental thinkers may be viewed by pro-NFP Catholics as logically inconsistent in their advocacy of the "natural" and nonviolent in a myriad of habitats as they maintain a laissez-faire attitude toward abortion and/or artificial contraception in the clinic and bedroom.

Whatever turn the population discussion takes, it has to be noted, in summary, that the Catholic magisterium has begun, in the decades since Vatican II, to develop and detail a theology of creation, an anthropology which understands the human in relation to the "web of life," and a visional ethic which is more profoundly aware of animals and ecosystems than earlier Catholic moral thinking has been. A prudent, just, temperate, and, as Cardinal Keeler half-joked, ecologically sensitive approach to living in the natural world is enjoined upon believers. Significant statements about the integrity of creation, the "ecological question," and the "ultimate pro-life issue" have appeared. These statements conform, it seems, to the models of "visional ethics" and "virtue ethics" associated with Stanley Hauerwas and Alasdair MacIntyre[25] and described by Craig Dykstra and John Crossin.[26] They also reflect, much more than initially meets the eye, Catholicism's Thomistic tradition. What remains to be seen is how well the magisterium can continue to dialogue with and attend to the insights of the widely varied schools of environmental ethical thought—those represented in this book, others already developing, and those still to be founded.

8
Conclusion

As severe hurricanes, tornadoes, snowstorms, floods, forest fires, and drought continue to afflict numerous regions of planet Earth, weatherwatchers continue to wonder how many of our climatic ills are human-induced. As they reflect on the disappearances of forests and rare species and the proliferation of contaminants in air, water, and soil, environmental thinkers of a variety of "schools" arrive at some convergence, but also much divergence, in their conclusions concerning the ethical implications of the plight of planetary health.

The movement toward some convergence among deep ecologists, ecofeminists, animal rights theorists, environmental holists (the "naturalists"), liberation ecotheologians, and religious ethicists is both heartening and noteworthy. As observed in the introductory pages of this text, there is virtual unanimity about the worthiness of the pursuit and promotion of environmental "sustainability"—as long as it is understood that "sustainability" is not maintenance of the status quo but, rather, deliberate sustenance of the natural environment in keeping with its optimal functioning and "integrity."

There seems, too, to be agreement that an egoistic, short-sighted anthropocentrism merits no credence. The perception that the abundance of creation exists merely to satisfy human need and whim is largely discredited. Environmental thinkers in general seem to identify as vice, crime, and/or sin a flagrant human disregard for pain inflicted on sentient animals. They also judge the wastage, toxification, and destruction inflicted on living things and their ecosystemic supports to be not only clear and present danger but also moral wrongs.

An ethic of human responsibility that acknowledges "interests" and well-being beyond the human realm seems clearly emergent. In some cases, the focus is described as more "biocentric"; in others, "biospheric" or "ecocentric"; and in some, both biocentric and ecocentric. For some, the anthropocentric is displaced by a more broadly "zoocentric" view. For others, anthropocentrism gives way to a more theocentric reverence for creation. For still others, a kind of "anthropoapical" view persists (as in Holmes Rolston), but in such a way that ecological considerations must be factored heavily into human decisions.

With the dislodging of a narrow anthropocentrism has come too a near consensus that "moral considerability" is due beings beyond *homo sapiens*. There is no agreement about whether talk of "rights" is beneficent or appropriate, but "rights" are commonly, and sometimes quite casually, invoked in environmental discussion. There seems to be abroad a general concession that the good of animals, of forests, of bioregions, of ecosystems, and of individual species must be weighed by human moral agents as they make decisions concerning personal practice and public policy.

An ethic of respect, if not of widespread "rights," seems to be arising from a conviction that some sort of "intrinsic value" can be posited for all sorts of lifeforms and their support systems. The basis for claiming such "intrinsic value" may be a religious one—a sense that creation, in all its diversity, is revelatory, bearing a "trace of the Trinity" (St. Thomas Aquinas, ST I.45.7) or God's "insignia," the "marks of his glory" (John Calvin, Institutes, I.v.1).[1] Or it may be an intuition of a kind of "spirit" or sacrality present in living creatures beyond the human. In a more philosophical vein, "intrinsic value" can be claimed on the basis of the directionality, the impetus to survival and continuation and proliferation which is observed among a wide array of living beings. Perceptions of "kinship" among the diversity of beings and of "interrelatedness" implicit in ecosystemic processes lend support to more evolutionary and cosmogenetic theories of "intrinsic value."

Philosophical arguments continue to rage about whether or how not yet existent beings might be said to make claims on present humans.[2] Nevertheless, speakers for most schools of environmental thought, with the possible exception of animal liberationists who focus quite strictly on the already existent, seem to take as axiomatic an obligation on the part of present humans to hand on to future generations of humans and other living beings a world capable of sustaining life and providing for some degree of flourishing.

The convergent themes in environmental ethics seem, then, to be largely visional. There is a move away from narrow anthropocentrism toward a more inclusive perception of "intrinsic value" and "moral considerability." There is a shift from a more mechanistic view of the natural world and a fixation on its elements' potential usefulness and service to humans toward a more relational, reverential attitude which allows for wise use but promotes more harmonious interaction. There seems too to be a correction of ethical myopia to a more panoramic view of behaviors and their environmental impact, immediate but also long-term.

While the desirable ends of environmental ethics seem readily describable (minimizing suffering for the sentient, assuring the possibility of surviving and thriving for hosts of species and ecosystems, calling a halt to wanton use and abuse, and taking steps to prevent ecological disasters), it is difficult to derive many specific prescriptions which the varied voices might agree on. Pleasantries are set forth as norms: "think globally, act locally"; engage in "thinking like a mountain"[3] and "listening to the land";[4] revere wildness and protect wilderness; learn ways of "living lightly" by simplifying lifestyles and resisting consumerism; develop new "nonaggressive and synergistic ways of living";[5] embody the truth that "small is beautiful."[6] All of these would seem unlikely to be confuted by the ecologically conscious. But how they are to be implemented and enfleshed is another question.

As should be clear from the foregoing chapters, there is considerable disagreement among environmental ethicists about whether or not any hierarchy of value or of preferential treatment should be allowed on the basis of species, place on the food chain, sentience, or capacity for reason. There is great disparity of opinion about who or what might hold "rights" and about whether rights-talk has any value at all in environmental ethical discussion. There is no ready agreement about how aggressively the preservation of species ought to be pursued or how much technology and "development" ought to be challenged and resisted.

There is also a great divide between those who would hope to attain "sustainable" societies through motivation and inspiration, attitude change, voluntary participation and those who would enact strict environmental legislation, set up extensive measures of enforcement, and impose severe penalties on violators. Questions of human population and tactics for containing its growth continue to seem incapable of resolution.

Profound entrenchments in culture, ideology, and customary patterns of thought (including those patterns which incline to racism, sexism, classism, "speciesism") lend themselves to little arbitration. The degree of attitudinal change to be sought from individuals and the degree of behavioral change to be exacted from societies are points of contention among the varying schools of environmental thought. Meat eating, road building, clearcutting of forests, chemical fertilizing, waste dumping, fossil fuel burning are all well established in a significant number of areas of the world. Patriarchal structures, the idealization of the bearing of male children, and treating some species of flora and fauna as desirable and others as undesirable are too. The pursuit of wealth, comfort, and technological ease has become virtually global. Deliberate choices for lower income, a lower standard of living, and less environmental impact are still likely to meet with derision and be perceived as fanatical.

No approach to environmental ethics seems altogether capable of negotiating these complexities.

One thing that seems to be fairly clear, in terms of moral methodology, is that environmental ethicists foresee little time for working a proportionalist calculus of goods and harms. Many tend to the deontological, asserting certain duties and obligations which humans have to the Earth environment which provides them with life, beauty, and nurturance. If agreement about proposed "absolutes" and norms is not possible, there may at least be some hope for the expansion and further describing of a visional environmental ethic and an exploration of solid and salutary environmental virtues.[7]

Notes

Introduction

1. Cf. Eric Chivian, M.D., et al., eds. *Critical Condition: Human Health and the Environment* (Cambridge: MIT Press, 1993). The articles in this publication examine urban phenomena, water pollution, food contamination, exposure to toxic substances and radiation, ozone depletion and ultraviolet effects, and the ravages of warfare as they affect human quality of life and health.

2. Catholic Bishops' Conference of the Philippines, "What Is Happening to Our Beautiful Land?" (1988), in Sean McDonagh, *The Greening of the Church* (Maryknoll: Orbis Books, 1990), 214.

3. Cf., e.g., Lester R. Brown, *Building a Sustainable Society* (New York: W. W. Norton and Company, 1981); the annual *State of the World* reports from Worldwatch (New York: W. W. Norton, issued each January); John Cobb, Jr., *Sustainability: Economics, Ecology, and Justice* (Maryknoll: Orbis Books, 1992); the account of the World Council of Churches' efforts in Wesley Granberg-Michaelson, "Creation in Ecumenical Theology," in David G. Hallman, ed., *Ecotheology: Voices from South and North* (Maryknoll: Orbis Books, with World Council of Churches Publications, 1994), 96–106; and "Liberating Life: A Report to the World Council of Churches," in Charles Birch, William Eakin, Jay B. McDaniel, eds., *Liberating Life: Contemporary Approaches to Ecological Theology* (Maryknoll: Orbis Books, 1990), 273–290.

4. Al Gore, *Earth in the Balance: Ecology and the Human Spirit* (New York: Houghton Mifflin, 1992), 12.

5. The essay, which originally appeared in *Ethics: An International Journal of Social, Political, and Legal Philosophy* 85 (1975), is included in Holmes Rolston III, *Philosophy Gone Wild: Essays in Environmental Ethics* (Buffalo: Prometheus Books, 1986), 12–29.

6. Joseph R. Des Jardins, *Environmental Ethics: An Introduction to Environmental Philosophy* (Belmont, CA: Wadsworth Publishing Company, 1993), 8.

7. Van Rensselaer Potter, *Global Bioethics: Building on the Leopold Legacy* (East Lansing: Michigan State University Press, 1988), 4.

1. Deep Ecology and Its Radical Vision

1. Alan Drengson and Yuichi Inoue, in their "Introduction" to *The Deep Ecology Movement: An Introductory Anthology* (Berkeley: North Atlantic Books, 1995), make a distinction between the philosophical premises of "deep ecology" and the "grass-roots...social and political movement" with which it is associated (xxi).

2. Cf. George Sessions, "Arne Naess and the Union of Theory and Practice," in Drengson and Inoue, 60.

3. Arne Naess, *Ecology, Community and Lifestyle,* trans. and rev. by David Rothenberg (New York: Cambridge University Press, 1989), 20.

4. Rothenberg, "Introduction," in Naess, *Ecology, Community, and Lifestyle,* 2.

5. Naess, *Ecology, Community and Lifestyle,* 37.

6. Rothenberg, in Naess, *Ecology, Community and Lifestyle;* also Naess, same text, 61.

7. Naess, *Ecology, Community and Lifestyle,* 32.

8. Naess, *Ecology, Community and Lifestyle,* 138–139.

9. Arne Naess, "Identification as a Source of Deep Ecological Attitudes," in *Deep Ecology,* ed. Michael Tobias (San Marcos: Avant Books, 1988), 266.

10. Bill Devall and George Sessions, in *Deep Ecology: Living as If Nature Mattered* (Salt Lake City: Gibbs M. Smith, 1985), identify "self-realization" as the first of two "ultimate norms or intuitions" in Naess' philosophy. The second they call "biocentric equality" (66).

11. Arne Naess, "Systematization of Logically Ultimate Norms and Hypotheses of Ecosophy T," in Drengson and Inoue, 45.

12. Naess treats these norms as nonabsolute. They are subject to what he calls "a principle of revisability." Cf. Naess, *Ecology, Community and Lifestyle,* 69.

13. Naess, in Drengson and Inoue, 33, 35, 43, 45.

14. Naess, in Tobias, 257.

15. Arne Naess, in "The Shallow and the Deep, Long-Range Ecology Movements: A Summary," in *Deep Ecology for the 21st Century,* ed. George Sessions (Boston: Shambhala, 1995), describes "the equal right to live and blossom" as "an intuitively clear and obvious value axiom" which applies broadly to living species. The application of the "equality" principle to humans only has had, Naess asserts, "detrimental effects upon the life quality of humans themselves" (152). The need to enact the principle across species boundary lines seems self-evident to Naess.

16. See Naess's discussion of relationality and gestalt in *Ecology, Community and Lifestyle,* 47–63.

17. Naess, in Drengson and Inoue, 35.

18. Naess, *Ecology, Community and Lifestyle,* 6.

19. Rothenberg, 11.

20. Rothenberg, 16–20.

21. Cf. Rothenberg, 5–6.

22. Cf. James E. Lovelock, *Gaia: A New Look at Life on Earth* (New York: Oxford University Press, 1979; reprint, 1987) and Anthony Weston, "Forms of Gaian Ethics," *Environmental Ethics* 9 (1987): 217–230.

23. Naess, *Ecology, Community and Lifestyle,* 23.

24. Naess, in Tobias, 257.

25. Naess, in Drengson and Inoue, 35.

26. The platform in full form can be found in Warwick Fox, *Toward a Transpersonal Ecology: Developing New Foundations for Environmentalism* (Boston: Shambhala, 1990), 114–115, and in numerous other deep ecology collections.

27. Confrontations have been regularly reported in the news media. Rationales for destructive "eco-defense" tactics have appeared in Edward Abbey's essay collection *One Life at a Time, Please* (New York: Henry Holt, 1988), 166, and, in a more picaresque and ambiguous way, in his novel *The Monkey Wrench Gang* (New York: Avon Books, 1975).

28. See the treatment of progress, technology, and population, for example, in Naess, *Ecology, Community and Lifestyle,* 23–32, 87–103, 140–141.

29. Stephan Bodian, "Simple in Means, Rich in Ends: An Interview with Arne Naess," in Sessions, ed., 27–28, 31–32.

30. This comment, which appeared in an EarthFirst! publication is quoted in Carolyn Merchant, *Radical Ecology: The Search for a Livable World* (New York: Routledge, 1992), 175.

31. Gore, 217.

32. The episode is told in fuller form in Roderick Nash, "Rounding Out the American Revolution: Ethical Extension and the New Environmentalism," in Tobias, 175.

33. Naess, in Tobias, 266.

34. Paul W. Taylor, "In Defense of Biocentrism," *Environmental Ethics* 5 (1983): 242–243.

35. Naess, in Tobias, 266.

36. "Rights," according to the understanding of Roderick Frazier Nash, are predicated simply on "intrinsic worth which humans ought to respect." See his *The Rights of Nature: A History of Environmental Ethics* (Madison: University of Wisconsin, 1989), 4.

37. Christopher D. Stone, *Should Trees Have Standing? Toward Legal Rights for Natural Objects* (Los Altos: W. Kaufman, 1974).

38. Nash, 7 (fig. 2) and 13.

39. Nash, 39–40, 66, 174.

40. John Tallmadge, "Saying You to the Land," *Environmental Ethics* 3 (1981): 353. It should be noted here that Tallmadge identifies himself as a Leopoldian, not as a disciple of Naess. He is included in this discussion of deep ecology rather than in Chapter 4's treatment of the "naturalist" school because his "I-You" theory is actually much closer to Naess's Ecosophy T than to Leopold's "land ethic."

41. Tallmadge, 354.

42. Tallmadge, 357.

43. Such a discipline will achieve, Tallmadge believes, four outcomes: 1) the seeker "confronts the being in its entirety" and "is impressed by its uniqueness"; 2) he or she senses in nature and any of its beings "a unique history, actualizing itself in time and space the same as he [or she]"; 3) the seeker becomes aware that each being "grows in a particular way," and 4) "bodies itself forth wholly in its own terms." For

Tallmadge, a disciplined attentiveness is the prerequisite to a "relational event" (360–361).

44. John Kultgen, "Saving You for Real People," *Environmental Ethics* 4 (1982): 63.

45. Kultgen, 65–66.

46. Tallmadge, 362.

47. Tallmadge, 363.

48. William C. French, "Against Biospherical Egalitarianism," *Environmental Ethics* 17 (1995): 39.

49. French, 40–41.

50. Peter S. Wenz, *Environmental Justice* (Albany: State University of New York Press, 1988), 340.

51. See, as a mid-1990s sampling, their works among those collected in *Deep Ecology for the 21st Century,* ed. George Sessions.

52. Fox, 197.

53. Fox, 200.

54. Fox, 245.

55. See Naess, "The Place of Joy in a World of Fact," in Sessions, ed., 249–258, and articles by Jack Turner, Thomas Birch, George Sessions, Edward Grumbine, Arne Naess, and Gary Snyder in Parts Five and Six of Sessions, ed.

56. Henryk Skolimowski, *Eco-Philosophy: Designing New Tactics for Living* (Boston: Marion Boyars, 1981), 12.

57. Skolimowski, 18, 22.

58. See Skolimowski's exposition of the characteristics of his eco-philosophy, 28–52.

59. Skolimowski, 77.

60. Skolimowski, 84.

61. Skolimowski, 112.

62. Bryan G. Norton, "Environmental Ethics and Weak Anthropocentrism," *Environmental Ethics* 6 (1984): 131–148.

63. Thomas Sieger Derr, with James A. Nash and Richard John Neuhaus, *Environmental Ethics and Christian Humanism* (Nashville: Abingdon Press, 1996), 22.

64. Derr, 32.

65. Derr, 100.

66. Cf. Warwick Fox, "The Deep Ecology-Ecofeminism Debate and Its Parallels," in Sessions, ed., 269–289, esp. 277–284.

2. The Ethics of Ecofeminism

1. Considerations of the desacralization of nature and the need for a recovery of a sense of the sacred pervade the following: Carol J. Adams, ed., *Ecofeminism and the Sacred* (New York: Continuum, 1993); Irene Diamond and Gloria Feman Orenstein, eds., *Reweaving the World: The Emergence of Ecofeminism* (San Francisco: Sierra Club Books, 1990); Judith Plant, ed., *Healing the Wounds: The Promise of Ecofeminism* (Philadelphia: New Society Publishers, 1989); Eleanor Rae, *Women, the Earth, the Divine* (Maryknoll: Orbis Press, 1994). Specifically Christian reflections on the ecocrisis, creation, and the sacred are found in: Catharina J. M. Halkes, *New Creation: Christian Feminism and the Renewal of the Earth,* trans. Catherine Romanik (Louisville: Westminster/John Knox Press, 1991); Elizabeth Johnson, *Women, Earth, and Creator Spirit* (New York: Paulist Press, 1991) and "The Cosmos: An Astonishing Image of God," *Origins* 26 (1996): 206–212; Anne Primavesi, *From Apocalypse to Genesis: Ecology, Feminism and Christianity* (Minneapolis: Fortress Press, 1991).

2. Karen J. Warren, "The Power and the Promise of Ecological Feminism," *Environmental Ethics* 12 (1990): 125. Carol Adams indicates the term's first appearance in French in 1972 (Adams, xi).

3. Warren, 125, 131.

4. Warren, 141, and Mary Ann Hinsdale, "Ecology, Feminism, and Theology," *Word and World* 11 (1991): 157, among others.

5. Ariel Salleh, "Deeper Than Deep Ecology: The Eco-Feminist Connection," *Environmental Ethics* 6 (1984): 340–344.

6. Carolyn Merchant, *The Death of Nature: Women, Ecology and the Scientific Revolution* (San Francisco: Harper Collins, 1980), xvi.

7. Merchant, 206.

8. She notes, for example, the subordinationist attitudes toward women which pervade the Aristotelian-Thomist system and appear in medieval and Renaissance poetry and art.

9. Merchant, 79–98.

10. Merchant, 294.

11. Merchant, 253–274.

12. Merchant's subsequent books include *Ecological Revolutions: Nature, Gender, and Science in New England* (Chapel Hill: University of

North Carolina Press, 1989) and *Radical Ecology: The Search for a Livable World* (New York: Routledge, 1992).

13. Merchant, *Radical Ecology*, 235–236.

14. Merchant, *Radical Ecology*, 237.

15. Merchant, *Radical Ecology*, 183, 185, 200–202.

16. Sallie McFague, *Metaphorical Theology: Models of God in Religious Language* (Philadelphia: Fortress Press, 1982), 5–6.

17. McFague, x–xii, 1–7.

18. McFague, 16–17. For McFague "a model is a dominant metaphor, a metaphor with staying power" (23).

19. When speaking of the model of God as mother, she notes that there is something to be gained by considering God "in the capacity, character, or role of mother" even while one is altogether aware that "God as mother" implies that God is and is not mother. Cf. Sallie McFague, *Models of God: Theology for an Ecological, Nuclear Age* (Philadelphia: Fortress Press, 1987), 23.

20. McFague, *Metaphorical Theology*, x–xi, and her general discussion of feminist theology, 147–177.

21. McFague, *Models of God*, 69–78.

22. Sallie McFague, *The Body of God: An Ecological Theology* (Minneapolis: Fortress Press, 1993), vii–viii.

23. McFague, *The Body of God*, 9.

24. McFague, *The Body of God*, 187. McFague presumes this throughout her work without entering into disputation over "rights" or matters of "intrinsic" vs. "instrumental" value. As mentioned in the introduction to this chapter, McFague, typical of ecofeminists, speaks more frequently of relationship and relatedness and generally refrains from rights-talk.

25. McFague, *The Body of God*, 20.

26. McFague, *The Body of God*, 22.

27. McFague, *The Body of God*, 24.

28. McFague, *The Body of God*, 37–39.

29. McFague, *The Body of God*, 48.

30. McFague, *The Body of God*, 49–55.

31. McFague, *The Body of God*, 197.

32. McFague, *The Body of God*, 59.

33. McFague, *The Body of God*, 200.

34. McFague, *The Body of God*, 202.

35. McFague, *The Body of God,* 200.

36. Rosemary Radford Ruether, *Gaia and God: An Ecofeminist Theology of Earth Healing* (San Francisco: Harper Collins, 1992), 31.

37. Ruether, 31.

38. Cf. Ruether, 199–201, 229–255.

39. Ruether, 39

40. Ruether, 256. See her treatment of possible outcomes of a correct visional ethic, 254–274.

41. For fuller description of these three "elements" of right relations—locality, extensive rights, and solidarity—see Ruether, 201.

42. The elaboration of all these goals and strategies appears in Ruether, 254–274.

43. Rosemary Radford Ruether, "Introduction," in *Women Healing Earth: Third World Women on Ecology, Feminism, and Religion* (Maryknoll: Orbis Books, 1996), 1.

44. Ruether, "Introduction," *Women Healing Earth,* 5.

45. Ruether, "Latin America," in *Women Healing Earth,* 12.

46. Ruether, "Asia," in *Women Healing Earth,* 64.

47. Ruether, "Africa," in *Women Healing Earth,* 118–119.

48. Rachel L. Bagby, "Daughters of Growing Things," in Diamond and Orenstein, eds., 231–248.

49. Carol Lee Sanchez, "Animal, Vegetable, and Mineral," in Adams, ed., 207–228.

50. Lina Gupta, "Ganga: Purity, Pollution, and Hinduism," in Adams, ed., 99–116.

51. See my essay on Dillard's works: Pamela A. Smith, "The Ecotheology of Annie Dillard: A Study in Ambivalence," *Cross Currents* 45 (1995): 341–358.

52. Linda L. Smith, *Annie Dillard* (New York: Twayne Publishers, 1991), 37–40.

53. Austin's narrative, reprinted in 1988 by Penguin Books, tells, with close attention to the Native American traditions and experience, tales of the terrain of the American West, particularly the stretch between the Sierras and Death Valley.

54. See Anne M. Clifford, "Feminist Perspectives on Science: Implications for an Ecological Theology of Creation," in Mary Heather MacKinnon and Moni McIntyre, eds., *Readings in Ecology and Feminist*

Theology (Kansas City: Sheed and Ward, 1995): 334–360, with comments on McClintock's principle on 345–346.
    55. Ruether, *Gaia and God,* 255.
    56. Salleh, 345.
    57. Fox, in Sessions, ed., 275–276.
    58. Donald Davies, "Ecosophy: The Seduction of Sophia," *Environmental Ethics* 8 (1986): 157, 160.
    59. Ruether, *Gaia and God,* 152, 155.
    60. Ruether, *Gaia and God,* 147.
    61. Ruether, *Gaia and God,* 147, 151–152. Ruether resists assigning certain attributes such as nurturance and magnanimous, other-oriented good will to the very essence of women and nature.
    62. Ruether, *Gaia and God,* 171. Daly is well known for her anti-male treatises. Her book *Gyn/Ecology: The Metaethics of Radical Feminism* (Boston: Beacon Press, 1978) considers cultural practices in which the violent subjugation of women seems to her to be allied to violence against nature (foot-binding in China, widow-burning in India, female circumcision in Africa). Daly's remedy for such subjugation and violation is the abandonment of all male systems and, to the extent possible, of men.
    63. Slicer mentions Fox's lack of serious attention to Karen Warren, Marti Kheel, Charlene Spretnak, and Ynestra King. She notes Ariel Salleh only in passing—as a minor figure. Cf. Deborah Slicer, "Is There an Ecofeminism-Deep Ecology Debate?" *Environmental Ethics* 17 (1995): 151–169.
    64. Slicer, 163.
    65. Slicer, 163.
    66. Slicer, 167–168, commenting on Val Plumwood's "Nature, Self, and Gender: Feminism, Environmental Philosophy and the Critique of Rationalism," *Hypatia* 6 (1991): 3–37.
    67. Slicer, 164.
    68. Michael E. Zimmerman, "Deep Ecology and Ecofeminism: The Emerging Dialogue," in Diamond and Orenstein, eds., 145.
    69. Zimmerman, 153–154.
    70. Zimmerman, 154.
    71. Marti Kheel, "Ecofeminism and Deep Ecology: Reflections on Identity and Difference," in Diamond and Orenstein, eds., esp. 134.
    72. Kheel, 137.

73. Cf., e.g., Carol J. Adams and Marjorie Proctor-Smith, "Taking Life or 'Taking on Life'? Table Talk and Animals," in Adams, ed., 295–310.

74. Kheel, 128.

3. Animal "Rights" and Questions of Human Behavior

1. Cf. Peter Singer, ed., *Ethics* (New York: Oxford University Press, 1994), 60–61, 67–69, 78–88, 93–95, 97–100.

2. Peter Singer, ed., *In Defence of Animals* (Oxford: Blackwell, 1985; rpt. 1991), 9.

3. Tom Regan, *The Case for Animal Rights* (Berkeley: University of California Press, 1983), 95. Despite some differences in their terms and premises, Regan (who speaks of "animal rights") and Singer (who prefers to speak of "animal liberation") attempt to locate their positions in a philosophical tradition which includes Bentham.

4. Regan, 31–32.

5. Lopez is best known for *Of Wolves and Men* (New York: Simon and Schuster, 1978) and *Arctic Dreams: Imagination and Desire in a Northern Landscape* (New York: Charles Scribner's Sons, 1986). The author's acute observations of animal behaviors and adaptations to their habitats provide not so much an ethical argument as an empirical one for their eliciting some sort of "compassionate regard," "enlightened respect," and a perception of their "intrinsic worth" from humans (cf. *Arctic Dreams,* 53, 113, e.g.).

6. Regan, 78, 116, 228.

7. Cf. Regan, 230, 263–265. Also cf. Tom Regan, *All That Dwell Therein: Animal Rights and Environmental Ethics* (Los Angeles: University of California Press, 1982), 94.

8. Regan, *The Case for Animal Rights,* 394–398.

9. Anthony J. Povilitis, "On Assigning Rights to Animals and Nature," *Environmental Ethics* 2 (1980): 67–71. Povilitis is here responding to the arguments against rights-holding for nonhumans leveled in Richard A. Watson, "Self-Consciousness and the Rights of Nonhuman Animals and Nature," *Environmental Ethics* 1 (1979): 99–129.

10. Tom Regan, "Introduction," in Tom Regan and Peter Singer, eds., *Animal Rights and Human Obligations* (Englewood Cliffs: Pren-

tice-Hall, 1976), 13. Also cf. Richard and Val Routley, "Against the Inevitability of Human Chauvinism," in K. E. Goodpaster and K. M. Sayre, eds., *Ethics and Problems for the 21st Century* (Notre Dame: University of Notre Dame Press, 1979), 36–59. James Rachels, in *Created from Animals: The Moral Implications of Darwinism* (Oxford: Oxford University Press, 1990), says (p. 181) that the term "speciesism" was coined by British psychologist Richard Ryder but brought into common parlance by Singer.

11. Regan, *The Case for Animal Rights*, 328.

12. In this section I have played out in detail a scenario suggested in a much more general way in Regan, *The Case for Animal Rights,* 327–328.

13. Tom Regan, "Christianity and Animal Rights: The Challenge and the Promise," in Birch, Eakin, and McDaniel, eds., 76.

14. Rachels, 175. Rachels says that his view is Darwinian in its attentiveness to similarities between humans and other species.

15. Cf. Rachels, esp. 208–212.

16. Mary Midgley, *Beast and Man: The Roots of Human Nature* (New York: Routledge, 1978; rev. 1995), 359.

17. Mary Midgley, *Animals and Why They Matter* (Athens: University of Georgia Press, 1983), 23.

18. Midgley, *Animals and Why They Matter,* 91, 144–145.

19. Jay B. McDaniel, *Earth, Sky, Gods and Mortals* (Mystic: Twenty-Third Publications, 1990), 27.

20. McDaniel, 63–65.

21. McDaniel, 74.

22. Jay B. McDaniel, "A God Who Loves Animals and a Church That Does the Same," in Charles Pinches and Jay B. McDaniel, eds., *Good News for Animals? Christian Approaches to Animal Well-Being* (Maryknoll: Orbis Books, 1993), 75–102.

23. Note, e.g., the Aristotelian-Augustinian-Thomistic distinctions between animals and humans upheld in a discussion of rightful respect for animals in Peter Drum, "Aquinas and the Moral Status of Animals," *American Catholic Philosophical Quarterly* 66 (1992): 483–488.

24. A kind of sociopolitical "environmental optimism" is found in Gregg Easterbrook, in *A Moment on Earth: The Coming Age of Environmental Optimism* (New York: Viking, 1995). Easterbrook takes the position that "mind" is what evolution is all about, that "consciousness is what

matters most about life," such that massive ethical rethinking and reform on environmental matters (and presumably on the treatment of animals) may prove uncalled for.

25. Charles Pinches, "Each According to Its Kind: A Defense of Theological Speciesism," in Pinches and McDaniel, eds., 189.

26. Pinches, 188–195.

27. Pinches, 201–202.

28. Pinches, 200, 203.

29. Pinches, 200.

30. Pinches, 201–203.

31. Tom Regan, "Do Animals Have a Right to Life?" in Regan and Singer, eds., 204.

32. Regan, *The Case for Animal Rights,* 359–361.

33. Cf. Lawrence Johnson, for a discussion of moral agency in monkeys, in *A Morally Deep World: An Essay on Moral Significance and Environmental Ethics* (New York: Cambridge University Press, 1991), 73. Singer's *Ethics* book, with its section on "Primate Ethics," tends in the same direction.

34. Cf. Laura Westra, "Ecology and Animals: Is There a Joint Ethic of Respect?" *Environmental Ethics* 11 (1989): 215–230.

35. Luc Ferry, no partisan of "animal rights," notes the attitudinal influences of the movement on British youth and the "hot-button" effects on French presidential politics. Cf. Ferry, *The New Ecological Order,* trans. Carol Volk (Chicago: University of Chicago Press, 1995), 19–21.

36. Comment on this Kenyan turn of events appears in Theodore Walker, Jr., "African-American Resources for a More Inclusive Liberation Theology," in Pinches and McDaniel, 164.

37. Linzey in particular emphasizes how the servant role of the human and the reconciling and liberating role of Christ might and should extend to a more compassionate regard for animals and to much more moral restraint in the uses to which they are put. A supporter of "Vegetarianism as a Biblical Ideal" and a critic of "Animal Experiments as Un-Godly Sacrifice" (chapter headings in the text cited here), Linzey advocates a decidedly less anthropo-focal liberation theology and urges that animals can be counted among the oppressed. Cf. Andrew Linzey, *Animal Theology* (Chicago: University of Illinois Press, 1994).

38. Mary Midgley, *Animals and Why They Matter,* 91.

4. The "Naturalists" and Leopoldian Ethics

1. Susan L. Flader, *Thinking Like a Mountain: Aldo Leopold and the Evolution of an Ecological Attitude toward Deer, Wolves, and Forests* (Columbia: University of Missouri Press, 1974), 31.

2. Leopold, in Susan L. Flader and J. Baird Callicott, eds., *The River of the Mother of God and Other Essays by Aldo Leopold* (Madison: University of Wisconsin Press, 1991), 44–45.

3. Flader and Callicott, eds., 94–96.

4. Flader and Callicott, eds., 191.

5. Flader and Callicott, eds., 268–269.

6. Flader and Callicott, eds., 270.

7. Aldo Leopold, *A Sand County Almanac and Sketches Here and There* (New York: Oxford University Press, 1949; rpt. 1989), viii.

8. Leopold, *A Sand County Almanac,* 109.

9. Leopold, *A Sand County Almanac,* 221.

10. Leopold, *A Sand County Almanac,* 204.

11. Leopold, *A Sand County Almanac,* 224–225.

12. Leopold, *A Sand County Almanac,* viii–ix.

13. J. Baird Callicott, "The Conceptual Foundations of the Land Ethic," in Callicott, ed., *Companion to "A Sand County Almanac": Interpretive and Critical Essays* (Madison: University of Wisconsin Press, 1987), 212.

14. Callicott, 205.

15. Callicott, 208.

16. J. Baird Callicott, *In Defense of the Land Ethic: Essays in Environmental Philosophy* (Albany: State University of New York Press, 1989), 240–242.

17. Lawrence E. Johnson, "Humanity, Holism, and Environmental Ethics," *Environmental Ethics* 5(1983): 345–354.

18. Cf. Lawrence E. Johnson, *A Morally Deep World,* esp. 6–7, 31, 94, 118ff. Also see Johnson, "Toward the Moral Considerability of Species and Ecosystems," *Environmental Ethics* 14 (1992): 145–157.

19. Johnson, *A Morally Deep World,* 142–146.

20. Johnson, *A Morally Deep World,* 173–195.

21. Johnson, *A Morally Deep World,* 256–257.

22. Alan Miller, *Gaia Connections: An Introduction to Ecology,*

Ecoethics, and Economics (Savage, MD: Rowman and Littlefield, 1991), esp. 249–253.

23. Robert Fuller, *Ecology of Care: An Interdisciplinary Analysis of the Self and Moral Obligation* (Louisville: Westminster/John Knox Press, 1992), esp. 63, 64, 72.

24. Wenz, 165.

25. Wenz, 235–250.

26. Wenz, 151–152.

27. Wenz, 272.

28. Wenz, 294–295.

29. Cf. Wenz's "Concentric Circle Perspective," 316–317.

30. Cf. Roderick Nash, "Aldo Leopold's Intellectual Heritage," in Callicott, ed., *Companion,* 63–84. Leopold is also cited a number of times in Nash's book.

31. Roderick Nash, *The Rights of Nature,* 4. See his schematic of expanding legal rights, Fig. 2, p. 7.

32. For a similar argument about the theoretical bases and the practical effects of environmental legislation and legal cases, recall Christopher Stone's *Should Trees Have Standing?* (noted in Chapter 1). Also cf., for another angle on the rights discussion, Alastair S. Gunn, "Environmental Ethics and Tropical Rain Forests: Should Greens Have Standing?" *Environmental Ethics* 16 (1994): 21–40.

33. Potter, *Global Bioethics,* esp. 59–60, 75, 129–179.

34. Rolston, *Philosophy Gone Wild,* 133.

35. Cf. Holmes Rolston III, *Environmental Ethics: Duties to and Values in the Natural World* (Philadelphia: Temple University Press, 1988), chaps. 2–5.

36. Rolston, *Environmental Ethics,* 73.

37. Rolston, *Environmental Ethics,* 71–73.

38. Rolston, *Environmental Ethics,* 254.

5. Liberation Ecotheology

1. Helder Camara, *Sister Earth: Creation, Ecology and the Spirit* (Hyde Park: New City Press, 1995), 26.

2. Gustavo Gutiérrez, *We Drink from Our Own Wells: The Spiri-*

tual Journey of a People, trans. Matthew J. O'Connell (Maryknoll: Orbis Books, 1984), 2.

3. Gutiérrez, 10.

4. Gustavo Gutiérrez, *The God of Life,* trans. Matthew J. O'Connell (Maryknoll: Orbis Books, 1991), 118–139, esp. 122.

5. Gutiérrez, *The God of Life,* 126.

6. Cf., e.g., Fernando Bermúdez, *Death and Resurrection in Guatemala,* trans. Robert R. Barr (Maryknoll: Orbis Books, 1986), where tales of disappearances and massacres and reflections on the paschal mystery lived by villages of tortured and slaughtered peoples are also tales of a "rich" land which became, in the 1970s and 1980s, the site of contaminated waters, poisoned forests and scorched fields.

7. Leonardo Boff, *Ecology and Liberation: A New Paradigm,* trans. John Cumming (Maryknoll: Orbis Books, 1995), 89.

8. Boff, 20–21.

9. Boff, esp. 25, 88.

10. Boff, 32, 93, 100–101, 105, 114.

11. Boff, 24.

12. Boff, 137.

13. Boff, 30, 89, 90.

14. Boff, 30.

15. Boff, 7, 25.

16. Boff, 38.

17. Boff, 128.

18. Boff, 86–87.

19. Boff, esp. 43–54.

20. Leonardo Boff, "Social Ecology: Poverty and Misery," in *Ecotheology: Voices from North and South,* ed. David G. Hallman, 246.

21. Cf. Thomas Berry, *The Dream of the Earth* (San Francisco: Sierra Club Books, 1988) and Brian Swimme and Thomas Berry, *The Universe Story* (San Francisco: Harper Collins, 1992).

22. Cf. Matthew Fox, *The Coming of the Cosmic Christ: The Healing of Mother Earth and the Birth of a Global Renaissance* (New York: Harper and Row, 1988) and *Creation Spirituality: Liberating Gifts for the People of the Earth* (San Francisco: Harper Collins, 1991).

23. Sean McDonagh, *The Greening of the Church,* 31–37, and *Passion for the Earth* (Maryknoll: Orbis Books, 1994), 75–82, 86–90.

24. Sean McDonagh, *To Care for the Earth: A Call to a New The-*

ology (Santa Fe: Bear and Company, 1986), 188–191. Cf. especially his passage on "biocide," 189–191.

25. McDonagh, *To Care for the Earth,* 190.

26. McDonagh, *The Greening of the Church,* 137.

27. McDonagh, *Passion for the Earth,* 127.

28. McDonagh, *Passion for the Earth,* 134.

29. McDonagh, *Passion for the Earth,* 124–146.

30. McDonagh, *Passion for the Earth,* 131.

31. McDonagh, *Passion for the Earth,* 130.

32. McDonagh, *Passion for the Earth,* 108.

33. McDonagh, *The Greening of the Church,* 137–138.

34. McDonagh, *Passion for the Earth,* 163.

35. McDonagh, *Passion for the Earth,* 147–161. Cf. also his "Liturgies of Earth and Fire" and "Celebrating Sacraments of Life" in *To Care for the Earth,* 154–168 and 169–186.

36. Merchant, *Radical Ecology,* 224–225.

37. McDonagh, *The Greening of the Church,* 198.

38. Boff, *Ecology and Liberation,* 30.

39. Dorothee Soelle, *On Earth as in Heaven: A Liberation Spirituality of Sharing,* trans. Marc Batko (Louisville: Westminster/John Knox Press, 1993), 89.

40. Robert McAfee Brown, *Liberation Theology: An Introductory Guide* (Louisville: Westminster/John Knox Press, 1993), 111.

41. R. M. Brown, 119.

42. Gibson Winter, *Liberating Creation: Foundations of Religious Social Ethics* (New York: Crossroad, 1981), x.

43. Kyle A. Pasewark, *A Theology of Power: Being Beyond Domination* (Minneapolis: Fortress Press, 1993), 320–336.

6. Eco-Ethics and the World's Religions

1. Hans Küng and Karl-Josef Kuschel, eds., *A Global Ethic: The Declaration of the Parliament of the World's Religions* (New York: Continuum, 1993), 14–15.

2. The wide-ranging list of the declaration's signers appears in Küng and Kuschel, eds., 37–39.

3. Küng and Kuschel, eds., 18, 24.

4. The bold print appears in the Küng and Kuschel text, 23.

5. The sum of what is considered under each of these directives appears in Küng and Kuschel, eds., 24–34.

6. Küng and Kuschel, eds., 16.

7. Küng, "The History, Significance and Method of the Declaration Toward a Global Ethic," in Küng and Kuschel, eds., 61–65.

8. Küng and Kuschel, eds., 22, 36.

9. Küng and Kuschel, eds., 26.

10. Küng and Kuschel, eds., 26.

11. Küng and Kuschel, eds., 26.

12. Küng and Kuschel, eds., 15.

13. For general comments on what might constitute change for the better in earthlings' behaviors, see Küng and Kuschel, eds., 36.

14. Tu Wei-Ming, "Beyond the Enlightenment Mentality," in Mary Evelyn Tucker and John A. Grim, eds., *Worldviews and Ecology: Religion, Philosophy, and the Environment* (Maryknoll: Orbis Books, 1994), 26.

15. Cf. Robert A. White, "A Baha'i Perspective on an Ecologically Sustainable Society," in Tucker and Grim, eds., 111.

16. Christopher Key Chapple, "Hindu Environmentalism," in Tucker and Grim, eds., 115, 117. Offering an explanation of the Jain perspective is deep ecologist Michael Tobias, in "Jainism and Ecology," in Tucker and Grim, eds., 138–149.

17. Brian Brown, "Toward a Buddhist Ecological Cosmology," in Tucker and Grim, eds., 125. For other treatments of Buddhist ecological perspectives, see Deane Curtin, "Dogen, Deep Ecology, and the Ecological Self," *Environmental Ethics* 16 (1994): 195–213, and Jay B. McDaniel, "Revisioning God and the Self: Lessons from Buddhism," in Charles Birch et al., eds., *Liberating Life,* 228–258.

18. Brian Brown, 127–128.

19. Cf., e.g., Huston Smith, "Tao Now: An Ecological Treatment," in Ian Barbour, ed., *Earth Might Be Fair* (Englewood Cliffs: Prentice-Hall, 1972), 62–81; Po-Keung Ip, "Taoism and the Foundations of Environmental Ethics," in Eugene C. Hargrove, ed., *Religion and Environmental Crisis* (Athens: University of Georgia Press, 1986), 94–106.

20. Mary Evelyn Tucker, "Ecological Themes in Taoism and Confucianism," in Tucker and Grim, eds., 151.

21. Tucker, 154–155.

22. Tucker, 158.

23. Roger E. Timm, "The Ecological Fallout of Islamic Creation Theology," in Tucker and Grim, eds., 88. Also cf. Iqtidar H. Zaidi, "On the Ethics of Man's Interaction with the Environment: An Islamic Approach," *Environmental Ethics* 3 (1981): 35–47.

24. Timm, 89.

25. For sample presentations concerning tribal religious attitudes toward the natural world, cf. Gerald Reed, "A Native American Environmental Ethic: A Homily on Black Elk," in Hargrove, ed., 25–37; Michael Kioni Dudley, "Traditional Native Hawaiian Environmental Philosophy," in Lawrence S. Hamilton with Helen Takeuchi, eds., *Ethics, Religion and Biodiversity* (Cambridge, UK: White Horse Press, 1993), 176–182.

26. Lynn White, Jr., "The Historical Roots of Our Ecologic Crisis," in Ian G. Barbour, ed., *Western Man and Environmental Ethics: Attitudes Toward Nature and Technology* (Reading, MA: Addison-Wesley Publishing Company, 1973), 24, 27.

27. Eric Katz, "Judaism and the Ecological Crisis," in Tucker and Grim, eds., 57.

28. Katz, 68.

29. Katz, 59.

30. Katz, 59–60.

31. H. Paul Santmire, *The Travail of Nature: The Ambiguous Ecological Promise of Christian Theology* (Minneapolis: Fortress Press, 1985), 218.

32. Wesley Granberg-Michaelson tells the story of the WCC's efforts in "Creation in Ecumenical Theology," in D. Hallman, ed., *Ecotheology*, 96–106.

33. Granberg-Michaelson, 99, 102.

34. Cf. "Liberating Life: A Report to the World Council of Churches," in Charles Birch et al., eds., 273–290.

35. "Liberating Life," 274.

36. René Coste, "The Ecumenical Dynamic of 'Justice, Peace and the Safeguarding of Creation,'" trans. John Bowden, in Johann Baptist Metz and Edward Schillebeeckx, *No Heaven Without Earth* (London: SCM Press, 1991), 27–28.

37. Larry Rasmussen, "Theology of Life and Ecumenical Ethics," in D. Hallman, ed., 118.

38. David G. Hallman, "Ethics and Sustainable Development," in D. Hallman, ed., 264.

7. Eco-Ethics and the Catholic Magisterium

1. Reported by the Catholic News Service, and quoted in "Holy Humor: Few Light Moments Surface at Bishops' Meeting," *Standard and Times,* 30 June 1995.

2. " Resources Offered to Help Parishes Relate Environment to Faith," *Catholic Witness,* 18 August 1995.

3. Drew Christiansen, S.J., and Walter Grazer, eds., *"And God Saw That It Was Good": Catholic Theology and the Environment* (Washington: United States Catholic Conference, 1996).

4. Pastoral Constitution on the Church in the Modern World, in Austin Flannery, O.P., ed., *Vatican Council II: The Conciliar and Post Conciliar Documents* (Northport, NY: Costello Publishing Company, 1992): 903–1001, cited in the text as GS with appropriate section numbers.

5. Cf. United States Catholic Conference, *Catechism of the Catholic Church* (Washington: USCC, 1994), #302. The "perfection of the universe" and the "perfections" creatures are discussed, e.g., in Thomas Aquinas' *Summa Contra Gentiles* II.45,1–10, and III.48.10, and in the *Summa Theologica* I.4.2, and I.5.3, as well as in other places.

6. John Paul II, *Redemptor Hominis (The Redeemer of Man)* (Boston: Daughters of St. Paul, 1979), #14. Cited hereafter as RH.

7. John Paul II, *Sollicitudo Rei Socialis (On Social Concerns),* in *Origins* 17 (3 March 1988), #26, #28. Cited hereafter as SRS.

8. John Paul II, *Centesimus Annus (On the Hundredth Anniversary of Rerum Novarum)* (Boston: St. Paul Books and Media, 1991), #31. Cited hereafter as CA.

9. John Paul II, *Veritatis Splendor (The Splendor of Truth),* in *Origins* 14 (1993), #1, #10, #12.

10. John Paul II, *Evangelium Vitae (The Gospel of Life)* (Boston: St. Paul Books and Media, 1995), #95. Cited hereafter as EV.

11. Al Gore has praised in particular the pope's 1990 World Day

of Peace message as "the most compelling, authoritative statement by a religious leader" on ecological matters. Cf. Patricia Zapor, "VP Cites Pope as 'Most Compelling' Religious Authority on Ecology," *Pittsburgh Catholic* (11 March 1994): 10. The message, "And God Saw That It Was Good," appears in *The Pope Speaks* 35 (1990): 200–206.

12. Catholic Bishops of the Philippines, in McDonagh, *The Greening of the Church*, 207–216, esp. 214–215.

13. National Conference of Catholic Bishops, "Renewing the Earth: An Invitation to Reflection and Action on the Environment in Light of Catholic Social Teaching," in *Origins* 21 (12 December 1991): 428–429.

14. NCCB, "Renewing," 429–430.

15. USCC, *Catechism*, #307, #373.

16. Joseph Des Jardins, in *Environmental Ethics,* describes "moral patients" as beings which "have moral standing.... They cannot act morally or not, but they can be acted on morally or immorally" (127).

17. Cf. NCCB, "Renewing," 426.

18. Cf. Richard Rohr, O.F.M., "Christianity and the Creation: A Franciscan Speaks to Franciscans," in Albert J. La Chance and John E. Carroll, eds., *Embracing Earth: Catholic Approaches to Ecology* (Maryknoll: Orbis Books, 1994): 129–155; also, Keith Warner, O.F.M., "Was Francis a Deep Ecologist?" in La Chance and Carroll, 224–240.

19. Cf. Terence Kardong, O.S.B., "Ecological Resources in the Benedictine Rule," in La Chance and Carroll, 163–173; also, René Dubos, "Franciscan Conservation versus Benedictine Stewardship," in David and Eileen Spring, eds., *Ecology and Religion in History* (New York: Harper and Row, 1974): 114–136.

20. Cf., e.g., Matthew Fox, *Sheer Joy: Conversations with Thomas Aquinas on Creation Spirituality* (San Francisco: Harper Collins, 1992). Two doctoral dissertations to date have pursued Thomistic eco-ethical connections: Jame Ehegartner Schaefer, "Ethical Implications of Applying Aquinas' Notions of Unity and Diversity of Creation to Human Functioning in Ecosystems," Ph.D. diss., Marquette University, 1994; and Pamela A. Smith, "Aquinas and Today's Environmental Ethics: An Exploration of How the Vision and the Virtue Ethic of 'Ecothomism' Might Inform a Viable Eco Ethic," Ph.D. diss., Duquesne University, 1995.

21. Potter, *Global Bioethics,* 50.

22. Albert La Chance identifies his position as a "new Catholic mysticism" in "Elucidating Catholic Values," in La Chance and Carroll, xxii. He makes strong anti-abortion comments in "God, the Cosmos, and Culture," in La Chance and Carroll, 16 and 23. Note also the endorsement of n.f.p. accompanied by a request for a reevaluation of the church's anti-contraceptive stance in David S. Toolan, S.J., "Open to Life—and to Death: The Church and Population Values," in La Chance and Carroll, 35–46.

23. Cf., e.g., Petra Kelly's "Foreword" in Judith Plant, ix; Catharina Halkes, 74; Carolyn Merchant, *Radical Ecology,* 199.

24. See Carolyn Merchant's discussion of Ariel Salleh in *Radical Ecology,* 104.

25. Cf. Stanley Hauerwas, *Vision and Virtue: Essays in Christian Ethical Reflection* (Notre Dame: Fides/Claretian, 1974) and Alasdair MacIntyre, *After Virtue: A Study in Moral Theory* (Notre Dame: University of Notre Dame Press, 1981) or MacIntyre, *Three Rival Versions of Moral Inquiry: Encyclopedia, Genealogy, and Tradition* (Notre Dame: University of Notre Dame Press, 1990).

26. Cf. Craig Dykstra, *Vision and Character: A Christian Educator's Alternative to Kohlberg* (New York: Paulist Press, 1981), and John W. Crossin, O.S.F.S., *What Are They Saying About Virtue?* (New York: Paulist Press, 1985).

8. Conclusion

1. *Calvin: Institutes of the Christian Religion,* ed. John T. McNeill (Philadelphia: Westminster Press, 1960), 2 vols.

2. See discussion in Bryan G. Norton, "Environmental Ethics and the Rights of Future Generations," *Environmental Ethics* 4 (1982): 319–337; also see Des Jardins, 72–95.

3. Recall the Leopold phrase and the Flader study cited in Chapter 4.

4. See the dialogues in Derrick Jensen, *Listening to the Land: Conversations about Nature, Culture, and Eros* (San Francisco: Sierra Club Books, 1995).

5. Jensen, 3.

6. This slogan is frequently borrowed from E. F. Schumacher, *Small Is Beautiful* (New York: Harper and Row, 1975).

7. See Geoffrey B. Frasz, "Environmental Virtue Ethics: A New Direction for Environmental Ethics," *Environmental Ethics* 15 (1993): 259–274; also, David Orr in Derrick Jensen, 29–30.

Bibliography

Abbey, Edward. *The Monkey Wrench Gang*. New York: Avon Books, 1975.
————. *One Life at a Time, Please*. New York: Henry Holt, 1988.
Adams, Carol J., ed. *Ecofeminism and the Sacred*. New York: Continuum, 1993.
Aquinas, Saint Thomas. *Summa Contra Gentiles*. 5 vols. Trans., with introductions by Anton G. Pegis, James F. Anderson, Vernon J Bourke, Charles J. O'Neil. New York: Doubleday and Company, 1955; reprint, Notre Dame: University of Notre Dame Press, 1975.
————. *Summa Theologica*. 5 vols. Trans. Fathers of the English Dominican Province. New York: Benziger Brothers, 1948; reprint, Westminster, MD: Christian Classics, 1981.
Barbour, Ian, ed. *Earth Might Be Fair*. Englewood Cliffs: Prentice-Hall, 1972.
————. *Western Man and Environmental Ethics: Attitudes Toward Nature and Technology*. Reading, MA: Addison-Wesley Publishing Company, 1973.
Bermúdez, Fernando. *Death and Resurrection in Guatemala*. Trans. Robert R. Barr. Maryknoll: Orbis Books, 1986.
Berry, Thomas. *The Dream of the Earth*. San Francisco: Harper Collins, 1992.
Birch, Charles, William Eakin, and Jay B. McDaniel, eds. *Liberating Life: Contemporary Approaches to Ecological Theology*. Maryknoll: Orbis Books, 1990.

Boff, Leonardo. *Ecology and Liberation: A New Paradigm.* Trans. John Cumming. Maryknoll: Orbis Books, 1995.

Brown, Lester R. *Building a Sustainable Society.* New York: W. W. Norton and Company, 1981.

Brown, Robert McAfee. *Liberation Theology: An Introductory Guide.* Louisville: Westminster/John Knox Press, 1993.

Callicott, J. Baird. *In Defense of the Land Ethic: Essays in Environmental Philosophy.* Albany: State University of New York Press, 1989.

Callicott, J. Baird, ed. *Companion to "A Sand County Almanac": Interpretive and Critical Essays.* Madison: University of Wisconsin Press, 1987.

Camara, Helder. *Sister Earth: Creation, Ecology and the Spirit.* Hyde Park: New City Press, 1995.

Catholic Bishops of the Philippines. "What Is Happening to Our Beautiful Land?" (1988), in Sean McDonagh, *The Greening of the Church*: 207–216.

Chivian, Eric, M.D., et al., eds. *Critical Condition: Human Health and the Environment.* Cambridge: MIT Press, 1993.

Christiansen, Drew, S.J., and Walter Grazer, eds. *"And God Saw That It Was Good": Catholic Theology and the Environment.* Washington: United States Catholic Conference, 1996.

Cobb, John, Jr. *Sustainability: Economics, Ecology, and Justice.* Maryknoll: Orbis Books, 1992.

Crossin, John W., O.S.F.S. *What Are They Saying About Virtue?* New York: Paulist Press, 1985.

Curtin, Deane. "Dogen, Deep Ecology, and the Ecological Self," *Environmental Ethics* 16 (1994): 195–213.

Daly, Mary. *Gyn/Ecology: The Metaethics of Radical Feminism.* Boston: Beacon Press, 1978.

Davies, Donald. "Ecosophy: The Seduction of Sophia," *Environmental Ethics* 8 (1986): 151–162.

Devall, Bill and George Sessions. *Deep Ecology: Living as If Nature Mattered.* Salt Lake City: Gibbs M. Smith, 1985.

Derr, Thomas Sieger, with James A. Nash and Richard John Neuhaus. *Environmental Ethics and Christian Humanism.* Nashville: Abingdon Press, 1996.

Des Jardins, Joseph R. *Environmental Ethics: An Introduction to Envi-*

ronmental Philosophy. Belmont, CA: Wadsworth Publishing Company, 1993.

Diamond, Irene and Gloria Feman Orenstein, eds. *Reweaving the World: The Emergence of Ecofeminism.* San Francisco: Sierra Club Books, 1990.

Drengson, Alan and Yuichi Inoue, eds. *The Deep Ecology Movement: An Introductory Anthology.* Berkeley: North Atlantic Books, 1995.

Drum, Peter. "Aquinas and the Moral Status of Animals," *American Catholic Philosophical Quarterly* 66 (1992): 483–488.

Dykstra, Craig. *Vision and Character: A Christian Educator's Alternative to Kohlberg.* New York: Paulist Press, 1981.

Easterbrook, Gregg. *A Moment on Earth: The Coming Age of Environmental Optimism.* New York: Viking, 1995.

Ferry, Luc. *The New Ecological Order.* Trans. Carol Volk. Chicago: University of Chicago Press, 1995.

Flader, Susan L. *Thinking Like a Mountain: Aldo Leopold and the Evolution of an Ecological Attitude toward Deer, Wolves, and Forests.* Columbia: University of Missouri Press, 1974.

Flader, Susan L. and J. Baird Callicott, eds. *The River of the Mother of God and Other Essays by Aldo Leopold.* Madison: University of Wisconsin Press, 1991.

Flannery, Austin, O.P., ed. *Vatican Council II: The Conciliar and Post Conciliar Documents.* Northport, NY: Costello Publishing Company, 1992.

Fox, Matthew. *The Coming of the Cosmic Christ: The Healing of Mother Earth and the Birth of a Global Renaissance.* New York: Harper and Row, 1988.

————. *Creation Spirituality: Liberating Gifts for the People of the Earth.* Maryknoll: Orbis Books, 1994.

————. *Sheer Joy: Conversations with Thomas Aquinas on Creation Spirituality.* San Francisco: Harper Collins, 1992.

Fox, Warwick. *Toward a Transpersonal Ecology: Developing New Foundations for Environmentalism.* Boston: Shambhala, 1990.

Frasz, Geoffrey. "Environmental Virtue Ethics: A New Direction for Environmental Ethics," *Environmental Ethics* 15 (1993): 259–274.

French, William C. "Against Biospherical Egalitarianism," *Environmental Ethics* 17 (1995): 39–57.

Fuller, Robert. *Ecology of Care: An Interdisciplinary Analysis of the Self and Moral Obligation.* Louisville: Westminster/John Knox, 1992.

Goodpaster, K. M. and K. E. Sayre, eds. *Ethics and Problems for the 21st Century.* Notre Dame: University of Notre Dame Press, 1979.

Gore, Al. *Earth in the Balance: Ecology and the Human Spirit.* New York: Houghton Mifflin, 1992.

Gunn, Alastair S. "Environmental Ethics and Tropical Rain Forests: Should Greens Have Standing?" *Environmental Ethics* 16 (1994): 21–40.

Gutiérrez, Gustavo. *The God of Life.* Trans. Matthew J. O'Connell. Maryknoll: Orbis Books, 1991.

————. *We Drink from Our Own Wells: The Spiritual Journey of a People.* Trans. Matthew J. O'Connell. Maryknoll: Orbis Books, 1984.

Halkes, Catharina J. M. *New Creation: Christian Feminism and the Renewal of the Earth.* Trans. Catherine Romanik. Louisville: Westminster/John Knox Press, 1991.

Hallman, David G., ed. *Ecotheology: Voices from South and North.* Maryknoll: Orbis Books, 1994.

Hamilton, Lawrence S. with Helen Takeuchi, eds. *Ethics, Religion and Biodiversity.* Cambridge, UK: White Horse Press, 1993.

Hargrove, Eugene C., ed. *Religion and the Environmental Crisis.* Athens: University of Georgia Press, 1986.

Hauerwas, Stanley. *Vision and Virtue: Essays in Christian Ethical Reflection.* Notre Dame: Fides/Claretian, 1974.

Hinsdale, Mary Ann. "Ecology, Feminism, and Theology," *Word and World* 11 (1991): 156–164.

Jensen, Derrick. *Listening to the Land: Conversations about Nature, Culture, and Eros.* San Francisco: Sierra Club Books, 1995.

John Paul II. "And God Saw That It Was Good," *The Pope Speaks* 35 (1990): 200–206.

————. *Centesimus Annus (On the Hundredth Anniversary of Rerum Novarum).* Boston: St. Paul Books and Media, 1991.

————. *Evangelium Vitae (The Gospel of Life)*. Boston: St. Paul Books and Media, 1995.

————. *Redemptor Hominis (The Redeemer of Man)*. Boston: Daughters of St. Paul, 1979.

————. *Sollicitudo Rei Socialis (On Social Concerns)*, in *Origins* 17 (1988): 641–660.

————. *Veritatis Splendor (The Splendor of Truth)*, in *Origins* 14 (1993): 297–334.

Johnson, Elizabeth. "The Cosmos: An Astonishing Image of God," *Origins* 26 (1996): 206–212.

————. *Women, Earth, and Creator Spirit*. New York: Paulist Press,1991.

Johnson, Lawrence. "Humanity, Holism, and Environmental Ethics," *Environmental Ethics* 5 (1983): 345–354.

————. *A Morally Deep World: An Essay on Moral Significance and Environmental Ethics*. New York: Cambridge University Press, 1991.

————. "Toward the Moral Considerability of Species and Ecosystems," *Environmental Ethics* 14 (1992): 145–157.

Küng, Hans and Karl-Josef Kuschel, eds. *A Global Ethic: The Declaration of the Parliament of the World's Religions*. New York: Continuum, 1993.

La Chance, Albert J. and John E. Carroll, eds. *Embracing Earth: Catholic Approaches to Ecology*. Maryknoll: Orbis Books, 1994.

Leopold, Aldo. *A Sand County Almanac and Sketches Here and There*. New York: Oxford University Press, 1949; reprint, 1989.

Linzey, Andrew. *Animal Theology*. Chicago: University of Illinois Press, 1994.

Lopez, Barry. *Arctic Dreams: Imagination and Desire in a Northern Landscape*. New York: Charles Scribner's Sons, 1986.

————. *Of Wolves and Men*. New York: Simon and Schuster, 1978.

Lovelock, James E. *Gaia: A New Look at Life on Earth*. New York: Oxford University Press, 1979; reprint, 1987.

MacIntyre, Alasdair. *After Virtue: A Study in Moral Theory*. Notre Dame: University of Notre Dame Press, 1981.

————. *Three Rival Versions of Moral Inquiry: Encyclopedia, Genealogy, and Tradition*. Notre Dame: University of Notre Dame Press, 1990.

MacKinnon, Mary Heather and Moni McIntyre, eds. *Readings in Ecology and Feminist Theology*. Kansas City: Sheed and Ward, 1995.

McDaniel, Jay B. *Earth, Sky, Gods and Mortals*. Mystic: Twenty-Third Publications, 1990.

McDonagh, Sean. *The Greening of the Church*. Maryknoll: Orbis Books, 1990.

————. *Passion for the Earth*. Maryknoll: Orbis Books, 1994.

————. *To Care for the Earth: A Call to a New Theology*. Santa Fe: Bear and Company, 1986.

McFague, Sallie. *The Body of God: An Ecological Theology*. Minneapolis: Fortress Press, 1993.

————. *Metaphorical Theology: Models of God in Religious Language*. Philadelphia: Fortress Press, 1982.

————. *Models of God: Theology for an Ecological, Nuclear Age*. Philadelphia: Fortress Press, 1987.

McNeill, John T., ed. *Calvin: Institutes of the Christian Religion*. Philadelphia: Westminster Press, 1960.

Merchant, Carolyn. *The Death of Nature: Women, Ecology and the Scientific Revolution*. San Francisco: Harper Collins, 1980.

————. *Ecological Revolutions: Nature, Gender, and Science in New England*. Chapel Hill: University of North Carolina Press, 1989.

————. *Radical Ecology: The Search for a Livable World*. New York: Routledge. 1992.

Metz, Johann Baptist and Edward Schillebeeckx, eds. *No Heaven without Earth*. London: SCM Press, 1991.

Midgley, Mary. *Animals and Why They Matter*. Athens: University of Georgia Press, 1983.

————. *Beast and Man: The Roots of Human Nature*. New York: Routledge, 1978; rev. 1995.

Miller, Alan. *Gaia Connections: An Introduction to Ecology, Ecoethics, and Economics*. Savage, MD: Rowan and Littlefield, 1991.

Naess, Arne. *Ecology, Community and Lifestyle*. Trans. and rev. by David Rothenberg. New York: Cambridge University Press, 1989.

Nash, Roderick Frazier. *The Rights of Nature: A History of Environmental Ethics*. Madison: University of Wisconsin Press, 1989.

National Conference of Catholic Bishops. "Renewing the Earth: An

Invitation to Reflection and Action on the Environment in Light of Catholic Social Teaching," in *Origins* 21 (1991): 424–432.

Norton, Bryan G. "Environmental Ethics and the Rights of Future Generations," *Environmental Ethics* 4 (1982): 319–337.

————. "Environmental Ethics and Weak Anthropocentrism," *Environmental Ethics* 6 (1984): 131–148.

Pasewark, Kyle A. *A Theology of Power: Being Beyond Domination.* Minneapolis: Fortress Press, 1993.

Pinches, Charles and Jay B. McDaniel, eds. *Good News for Animals? Christian Approaches to Animal Well-Being.* Maryknoll: Orbis Books, 1993.

Plant, Judith, ed. *Healing the Wounds: The Promise of Ecofeminism.* Philadelphia: New Society Publishers, 1989.

Plumwood, Val. "Nature, Self, and Gender: Feminism, Environmental Philosophy and the Critique of Rationalism," *Hypatia* 6 (1991):3–37.

Potter, Van Rensselaer. *Global Bioethics: Building on the Leopold Legacy.* East Lansing: Michigan State University Press, 1988.

Povilitis, Anthony. "On Assigning Rights to Animals and Nature," *Environmental Ethics* 2 (1980): 67–71.

Presbyterian Church (U.S.A). *Restoring Creation for Ecology and Justice.* Louisville: Presbyterian Church (U.S.A.), 1990.

Presbyterian Eco-Justice Task Force. *Keeping and Healing the Creation.* Louisville: Presbyterian Church (U.S.A.), 1989.

Primavesi, Anne. *From Apocalypse to Genesis: Ecology, Feminism and Christianity.* Minneapolis: Fortress Press, 1991.

Rachels, James. *Created from Animals: The Moral Implications of Darwinism.* Oxford: Oxford University Press, 1990.

Rae, Eleanor. *Women, the Earth, the Divine.* Maryknoll: Orbis Books, 1994.

Regan, Tom. *All That Dwell Therein: Animal Rights and Environmental Ethics.* Los Angeles: University of California Press, 1982.

————. *The Case for Animal Rights.* Berkeley: University of California Press, 1983.

Regan, Tom and Peter Singer, eds. *Animal Rights and Human Obligations.* Englewood Cliffs: Prentice-Hall, 1976.

Rolston, Holmes, III. *Environmental Ethics: Duties to and Values in the Natural World.* Philadelphia: Temple University Press, 1988.

―――. *Philosophy Gone Wild: Essays in Environmental Ethics.* Buffalo: Prometheus Books, 1986.

Ruether, Rosemary Radford. *Gaia and God: An Ecofeminist Theology of Earth Healing.* San Francisco. Harper Collins, 1992.

―――. *Women Healing Earth: Third World Women on Ecology, Feminism, and Religion.* Maryknoll: Orbis Books, 1996.

Salleh, Ariel. "Deeper Than Deep Ecology: The Eco-feminist Connection," *Environmental Ethics* 6 (1984): 339–345.

Santmire, H. Paul. *The Travail of Nature: The Ambiguous Ecological Promise of Christian Theology.* Minneapolis: Fortress Press, 1985.

Schaefer, Jame Ehegartner. *Ethical Implications of Applying Aquinas' Notions of Unity and Diversity of Creation to Human Functioning in Ecosystems.* Ph.D. diss., Marquette University, 1994.

Schumacher, E. F. *Small Is Beautiful.* New York: Harper and Row, 1975.

Sessions, George, ed. *Deep Ecology for the 21st Century.* Boston: Shambhala, 1995.

Singer, Peter, ed. *Ethics.* New York: Oxford University Press, 1994.

―――. *In Defence of Animals.* Oxford: Blackwell, 1985; reprint, 1991.

Skolimowski, Henryk. *Eco-Philosophy: Designing New Tactics for Living.* Boston: Marion Boyers, 1981.

Slicer, Deborah. "Is There an Ecofeminism-Deep Ecology Debate?" *Environmental Ethics* 17 (1995): 151–169.

Smith, Linda L. *Annie Dillard.* New York: Twayne Publishers, 1991.

Smith, Pamela A. *Aquinas and Today's Environmental Ethics: An Exploration of How the Vision and the Virtue Ethic of "Ecothomism" Might Inform a Viable Eco-Ethic.* Ph.D. diss., Duquesne University, 1995.

―――. The Ecotheology of Annie Dillard: A Study in Ambivalence," *Cross Currents* 45 (1995): 341–358.

Soelle, Dorothee. *On Earth as in Heaven: A Liberation Spirituality of Sharing.* Trans. Marc Batko. Louisville: Westminster/John Knox Press, 1993.

Spring, David and Eileen, eds. *Ecology and Religion in History.* New York: Harper and Row, 1974.

Stone, Christopher. *Should Trees Have Standing? Toward Legal Rights for Natural Objects.* Los Altos: W. Kaufman, 1974.

Swimme, Brian and Thomas Berry. *The Universe Story*. San Francisco: Harper Collins, 1992.

Tallmadge, John. "Saying You to the Land," *Environmental Ethics* 3 (1981): 351–363.

Taylor, Paul W. "In Defense of Biocentrism," *Environmental Ethics* 5 (1983): 237–243.

Tobias, Michael, ed. *Deep Ecology*. San Marcos: Avant Books, 1988.

Tucker, Mary Evelyn and John A. Grim, eds. *Worldviews and Ecology: Religion, Philosophy, and the Environment*. Maryknoll: Orbis Books, 1994.

United States Catholic Conference. *Catechism of the Catholic Church*. Washington: United States Catholic Conference, 1994.

Warren, Karen J. "The Power and the Promise of Ecological Feminism," *Environmental Ethics* 12 (1990): 125–146.

Watson, Richard A. "Self-Consciousness and the Rights of Nonhuman Animals and Nature," *Environmental Ethics* 1 (1979): 99–129.

Wenz, Peter S. *Environmental Justice*. Albany: State University of New York Press, 1988.

Weston, Anthony."Forms of Gaian Ethics," *Environmental Ethics* 9 (1987): 217–230.

Westra, Laura. "Ecology and Animals: Is There a Joint Ethic of Respect?" *Environmental Ethics* 11 (1989): 215–230.

Winter, Gibson. *Liberating Creation: Foundations of Religious Social Ethics*. New York: Crossroad, 1981.

Wright, Nancy G. and Donald Kill. *Ecological Healing: A Christian Vision*. Maryknoll: Orbis Books, 1993.

Zaidi, Iqtidar H. "On the Ethics of Man's Interaction with the Environment: An Islamic Approach," *Environmental Ethics* 3 (1981): 35–47.

Other Books in This Series